Nightmare of the Past

Amra Podrug Kratina

Joshua Tree
Publishing

• Chicago •

Nightmare of the Past
Amra Podrug Kratina

Published by
Joshua Tree Publishing
• Chicago •
JoshuaTreePublishing.com

13-Digit ISBN: 978-1-956823-38-7

Disclaimer:

This book is a memoir based on true events. It reflects the author's opinions and present recollections of experiences over time. Some events have been compressed, and some dialogue has been recreated. In order to maintain anonymity in some instances, the names of individuals have been changed, including some identifying characteristics and details such as physical properties, occupations, and places of residence. Neither the publisher nor the author shall be held liable or responsible for any loss or damage allegedly arising from any suggestion or information contained in this book.

Printed in the United States of America

Dedication

This book is dedicated to all women victims of the war in Bosnia and Herzegovina as well as to all victims from all over the world who have survived physical and psychological abuse.

Table of Contents

Prologue

The chilling water is making me cold. The crashing waves sound like a banshee to my ears. I keep splashing and waving my arms to reach the surface of the ocean. However, no matter how much I try, the waves keep pushing me back down into its arms. The ocean is not letting me escape from its embrace. The dark and gloomy gray clouds are angrily roaring above, shedding bitter tears into the ocean. Water keeps going in my lungs, making it impossible for me to breathe. The more I drown, the more the sunlight keeps dimming. But I want to survive. I want to live!

* * *

Such was my mental turmoil; I felt as if I would not survive the dark abyss of the world that my life had become. After going through so much pain and torture from the people who ruined my life, I finally made it to the shore in the end.

Life had always been hard on me. It kept playing with me and tormenting me, making me anxious and scared at every step of my life. Nevertheless, I did not lose hope and surrender myself into its evil trap. I freed myself from the hold it had on me.

Survival can be summed up in three words—never give up.
That's the heart of it, really. Just keep trying.
—Bear Grylls

My life in Bosnia was so gruesome that I don't even want to think of it anymore. It scares me to death when the episodes of my life in Bosnia flash before my eyes. I am no longer trapped there, but the memories linger on. As I share my harrowing journey with you, I admit it won't be easy for me to talk about it, but I have to face my fears and past demons and free myself. That is something I have learned by going through hell for years.

I am ready to tell you my life story, hoping it will inspire you to be bold and courageous and take control of your life. I have learned the hard way that in difficult times, people rarely come forward to help you. They fancy insulting and mocking you rather than sympathizing with you. All the hardships I went through were frightening and full of mishaps and anguish.

The most terrifying of these hardships was the unexpected death—or if I may say, the murder—of my father and the heartaches and sorrow of living my life without him. I remember the isolated time I spent with my family while a war was going on in Bosnia, my dreadful and painful life when the Serbs imprisoned me. The people and circumstances made it extremely hard for me to breathe. I was alive, but my soul was shattered. I was dreaming, but it was dark and empty—a nightmare in the making.

I was desperate for fresh air, for the love and warmth of my family, for my innocence. I was unable to fathom how to numb the pain; it was like thousands of needles were being pierced in my body at the same time, every day, all the time!

Whenever I remember that time and the things I had to go through in Bosnia, uncontrollable shivers roll down my body. I still remember those menacing faces when they used to beat me—the spine-chilling smirks of my tormentors when they had fun torturing me.

I gave up on the idea of surviving or being free again. My confidence level went down. I lost all hope of being happy again in this life. My will to fight back in that situation was long gone. Even when I was finally free from the clutches of my tormentors, I used to get scared of the whispers of the night while out on the street. I was frightened that someone or something would appear out of nowhere and pounce on me.

I used to wake up in the middle of the night, worried that I was still trapped in the tormentor's chains. Consequently, I had to undergo many therapy sessions to be where I am today, to reclaim my life as I desired. In fact, this is one of the very reasons I am writing this book: to tell you that we must not lose hope and let people know that we can still survive despite the sufferings they had put us in.

My own people did not help my situation; they did not make it easy for me. Their accusing eyes made me self-conscious. The way they scrunched their nose whenever I came across them made me feel insecure and disgusted with myself. Their mocking and insulting behavior was so traumatizing that it demoralized me a lot.

I could not understand how to let them know that I was not at fault—that I was a victim, not the other way around. As a result, I started treating myself in the worst possible way, loathing and blaming myself!

I started to think that whatever bad happened to me was my fault. I started believing what people were thinking about me was correct and that I deserved whatever life was throwing at me. All of it made my mental and emotional health unstable at that time. But not anymore!

I know the memories will forever haunt me, but I will not let them stop me from moving on! I don't care what the world thinks about me. Nobody will ever understand my pain as they do not know what I have been through. No more trembling in fear, no more nightmares and horrible flashbacks!

The worst days are gone for good! Now, only the blissful and sunny days are ahead, and penning down my story makes me feel more relaxed and calmer now. I want to share my story with people so they can know what went down in Bosnia. I feel more secure and happy that I am able to move forward from my past.

I don't want to be a scaredy-cat anymore, hiding in my shell and letting myself be tormented for the rest of my life.

No!

Never!

I am not scared of them anymore. I want to release the trauma and burden I have been lifting on my shoulder for so long. I wish to convey my story to everyone out there to help them understand that they can go through anything if they do not give up.

I love this quote from Rodney A. Winters, the author of *Go into the House*, as it inspires me and makes me feel proud of myself.

Scars are not signs of weakness;
they are signs of survival and endurance.

I am writing my story to let people know that even if life is at times difficult, one must not back down and lose confidence. We must think that there is a way to be successful and not let go of the rope of hope. Motivation and encouragement can lead us to fulfill what we want in our lives.

I want to help people overcome their sufferings and hardships by becoming an inspiration through this book. I want my story to help motivate them to move forward despite the problems and challenges in their life. I know it is not easy to do so, but it will be done when we are determined. It may take some time, but we will achieve what we desire somehow.

Nothing in this world is forever. Everything will become a part of the past someday, and our lives will be better again.

Chapter 1

The Lost Soul

A great soul serves everyone all the time. A great soul never
dies. It brings us together again and again.
—Maya Angelou

I have always heard that childhood is the best part of our life as most
of us are carefree then, but my childhood wasn't that good. I was forced
to grow up, leaving all my innocence behind; I was faced with a dreadful
life ahead.

In the blink of an eye, the beautiful bright-yellow color surrounding
my life turned into a dark, stormy gray. The dreams I have longed for
so many years were now far away from me. It wasn't the life I had ever
wanted; it wasn't something I could ever dream about.

Why?

Why did it happen?

The warmth of my father's arms was snatched away from me. The
protection and solicitude he gave me were taken away from me. It happened
so quickly that I did not have a chance to fight back. I was ten years old
when my life started to crumble. I was hit with a tragedy at such a young
age that made me feel powerless. My life became a nightmare when, one
day, my father went missing.

I got to spend too little time with my father—those moments are still
dear to my heart. My father was a handsome tall thirty-five-year-old man
with long brown hair that complemented his charm. He was born and bred
in a village, a canonist man who was fond of wearing suits.

My father was a supervisor in a factory; he earned enough for the family, so my mother didn't have to work. Everyone in our community and neighborhood loved him. He was supportive and caring and helped out my mother whenever possible. He always put effort into knowing what was going on in his kids' lives, and he even helped me do my schoolwork.

Perhaps the best thing about my father was that he had consistently kept an exceptionally protected and open environment in our house. My younger brother and I could discuss anything with him without worrying about being scolded or judged. This helped us not lie, which was one quality I frequently saw was missing in my friends.

Also, my father loved animals; he had an undying affection for them, making him highly thoughtful. I never saw my dad act mischievously with his brothers or my grandparents. He was a simple man who respected everyone and looked after them.

Dad was not only nice to us but everybody in general, regardless of whether or not he knew them. Whenever anyone needed any help and my father promised them something, he was always there to fulfill it. He was a respectful and caring individual, and others treated him the same way.

My father was a modest and calm person and never got into arguments. He always talked to people politely and affably. He treated people equally; for him, everyone was good and virtuous. His personality and nature always left me in awe of him, and he became my role model. I felt secure with him because he was the person who could save me from the evils of this world. He treated all children equally through his words and actions.

A father's presence in a child's life is like a green sepal that surrounds the bud before it becomes mature. The sepal protects the delicate bud so that it remains safe and does not get ripped apart from the harsh, cold wind. Just like sepal, a father is a backbone for the children—the backbone they can use to support themselves and cry and rest on in trying times.

* * *

I remember this incident when I clumsily hit my knee on the edge of the wooden table placed in the living room corner. I was crying hysterically, sitting on the floor with blood trickling down my leg, when my father appeared at the doorway.

The shallow breaths, panicked eyes, and emergency on his face could clearly describe how worried he was for me. One glance at me made him run toward me.

"Don't worry, my child, it's going to be all right." He tried to comfort me, but I was in so much pain that I could not hear him.

"Wait," my father said, rushing toward the cupboard on the left side of the room and taking out the first aid box. He made his way to me again and opened the box. "See, I am going to clean it now, child, don't cry." He poured some alcohol on the cotton bud and placed it on my knee.

"Ah!" I screamed in pain.

"Shh . . . ," my father soothed me. He said, "You are my bravest daughter, I know you can bear it. You are a strong child." He again and again tried to console me with his words. I believed him! His words impacted me, and I instantly calmed down.

My father noticed this change in me, sighed in relief, and then began to clean up my wound. After he was done, he placed a small Band-Aid on my knee, which made me giggle. He looked at me and beamed back, finding joy in watching me smile. Placing his arm around my shoulders and legs, he lifted me and started walking toward my bedroom on the first floor.

My parents decorated my room themselves with love. It was decorated with cream-colored paint on the walls and beautiful hanging lights on the ceiling. It was not only the adornment that could be seen in the room but also the love and dedication of my parents that was evident.

Being careful of my wound, my father placed me on my brown, round-shaped bed situated at the center of the room.

"Come on, it's time to sleep now," he said to me. He kept patting my head lightly until I was asleep.

* * *

My family lived in a city, but my father grew up in a village. My paternal grandparents still lived in the village even after my father had moved to the city. Though we lived far away, my father cared about his family immensely.

My grandparents, being old and weak, could not do hard labor, so my father visited them every summer to help them out with any work they needed assistance with. Every Friday after work, he would visit the village, stay there for the weekend, and come back home on Sunday.

It was supposed to go this way on that dreadful day too. Unfortunately, fate had something else planned for us! We could not have ever imagined that he would never come back to us this time or that it would be the last time we would see him.

My father left for work on Friday, saying, "Take good care of yourself and your mother. Do not give trouble to your mother, and I will be back on Sunday!" He promised us his return, smiling warmly and kissing our foreheads.

There was a twinkle in his eyes, the light that made you blink. Alas! My father did not know that this was the only promise he could never fulfill, no matter how hard he tried!

With a cheerful farewell, my father departed for his work. Two days flew by, and the day we were eagerly waiting for—Sunday—came. My siblings and I were looking forward to his return, eyes fixed on the front door, waiting.

We did not want to shift our eyes from the door for even a second, afraid that we would miss his smile as soon as he opened the door. His smile was contagious; he would light up the whole room with his cheerful smile.

We waited and waited.

Eleven o'clock.

Twelve midnight.

One o'clock.

My mother comforted us siblings. "It's okay, we do not have to worry. Maybe Grandpa and Grandma have a lot of work they need help with. Your father would come back early in the morning tomorrow if that is the case," she said, reassuring us and urging us to go to sleep.

"Okay, Mother," we said in unison, agreeing to obey her and going off to sleep thinking we would see our father in the morning.

Little did we know what fate had in store for us.

* * *

The next day, while we were having breakfast, the doorbell rang. My mother made her way to the front door, and excited, I followed her.

Father is finally back, I thought.

However, the door opened to reveal three men in black shirts and blue jeans who all greeted my mother. They introduced them as team leaders of the company where my father worked. They asked about my father's whereabouts. There was a strange feeling in the pit of my stomach as if something was not right, but what?

When my mother replied that she also did not know where he was, they asked if we had the keys to the company as no one was able to enter the company building because my father had the keys. My mom told them she did not have the keys. Perplexed, the team leaders went their way.

I was confused. I could not understand what was going on. My mother, however, was still not worried that something might be wrong; she was keen on the idea that everything was okay. She thought that maybe my father had stayed with his parents.

Mom's hope was what kept my siblings and me from getting disheartened. The whole day went by as we waited for my father, but he did not come. In the afternoon, my paternal aunt visited us. She worked at the same company as my father on the second shift.

"Where is your brother right now? Why didn't he go to work? Why did he have to stay?" My mother showered her with question after question.

"What are you even talking about? He left last night," my aunt replied, and it shocked my mother. My aunt kept repeating, "What is wrong?"

But my mother was not in a conscious state to say anything. It was then that we realized something was wrong.

Within an hour, many people, including my uncle, turned up at our house. After consoling my family and learning of what happened, they started to search for my father but could not find him.

My father was a kind and humble person; everyone in our neighborhood was worried for him. His office employees would visit to know if there was any update on him. The police, family, and friends continuously looked for him for three days. They spent days and nights searching every corner where he could be found, but to no avail. Nobody could find Dad.

My mother was upset, praying every minute for my father's well-being. She was not able to eat and sleep properly. She was in a state where sometimes I had to remind her of us. It was very difficult for me to see my family in that state.

My six-month-old brother needed my mother's care and attention, but she unconsciously neglected him since her attention was fixated on her husband's absence. My seven-year-old brother and I were lost; we were missing our father. We could not grasp why he was not there with us and didn't know where he was.

My house remained packed with people for three days when they were all searching for my father. On the fourth day, too, many people visited us. My mother thought it would be rude not to cater to them, so in the midst of it, she told me to buy *burek* from the bakery.

I remembered there were a lot of people in the bakery, and they were talking loudly. At first, I couldn't hear what they were talking about. I let it go, thinking it was not my concern. However, after a few minutes, a voice could be heard clearly.

"What?" a male voice shouted loudly. "What are you talking about?"

"Do you know the man people have been searching for for three days? His body was found in the river!" a second male voice shared loudly.

"Gosh, I couldn't believe it! What will happen to his family now? I heard he has three children too," the first voice murmured remorsefully.

"I know!" the second voice said. "Poor him! I feel bad for him and his family now . . ."

I was startled! I was numb!

The conversation carried on, but I didn't listen further. My mind was stuck on the person's sentence and the information it had: they had found a body and also near the river! The worst thing was that the person was missing.

Could it be? No! No way it could be him! Stop thinking horrible things! I scolded my mind from contemplating everything terrible. My father wouldn't leave us alone, he just can't. He loves us dearly, his life revolves around us. He wouldn't just leave us like that, I thought, fighting my own self.

My legs were stiff, as if someone had glued them to the floor. I took a deep breath and immediately ran back to my house to inform my mother what I had heard.

"Mom!" I yelled, running to her. "I . . . I want to tell you something important!"

"What is it?" my mother asked, embracing me.

My relatives were shocked; they immediately tried to calm me down.

"Calm down, child," my uncle murmured soothingly and caressed my head.

"No, no, I can't calm down. I think it is something related to Father. Mom . . . I heard . . ." I repeated to her what I had heard in the bakery.

My mother's face turned pale; it was as if she didn't know how to breathe anymore. I was afraid for a second, thinking I would be losing my mother too.

My uncle and aunt surrounded her, patting and stroking her to wake her up from the shock. They yelled and cried for her, requesting her to respond.

"Sister!" my aunt shouted, squeezing her hand. "Wake up, please!"

"Please!" my uncle screamed, shaking her shoulder forcefully. "Come back to your senses!"

One second passed.

Two seconds passed.

And then, Mom started crying, which also made my brother tear up. He ran toward my mother and hugged her legs. Hiding his face, he wept violently.

Gazing around, I could see that everyone in the living room was either crying or comforting my family. They were trying to calm us down, knowing that we had lost an important person in our life.

Everyone was crying besides me. I did not cry; not a single tear dropped from my eye that time, but my heart was clenching painfully. I was dazed, too shocked to understand what was going on. It felt like the light in my life had left me. I would no longer be seeing the light again; my world was submerged in darkness.

I went out of the house, wanting to be alone. I stayed outside most of the time as I wanted to mourn for my father alone. I was savoring his memories, remembering his words. I was trying to capture him, his face, his smile, and his love in my mind. I tried to remember the way he would call me and comfort me every time I failed, but it felt as if he was only vanishing into thin air. The more I tried to remember him, the further he got—or that was how I felt it was, at least.

After taking him out of the river, the medics did an autopsy on the body. They told my mother that my father was already dead before he was found in the river. Yet it was perceived and declared as a suicide case.

The police did some investigation and concluded in the report that my father committed suicide. My family and relatives wanted to investigate more, but nothing could be done after the police had given their conclusion.

It was hard to believe; we knew that my father could not commit suicide. He was a loving person who valued his life and family. He would never willingly abandon us. He loved us dearly. My mother and I kept living in that misconception, not knowing the actual reason behind his demise, only consoling and encouraging each other.

It was during the war that we learned a coworker killed my father in a bar. That coworker was our neighbor. His son went to school with my brother and me. The coworker was fighting with someone else, which got out of hand and turned violent. My father did not like violence; he got in the middle of them and tried to stop them. Unfortunately, his coworker hit my father instead of the person he was aiming at. Both of them panicked and put my father in one of their apartments for three days. When they saw everyone was looking for my father, they threw him into the river.

He lay there abandoned like a lost soul, as if he weren't a human being but something else. I wish it had never happened and my father were here with me. His death did not harm those people in any way, but it was a huge loss for my family!

To this day, I still wonder how people could be this heartless that they didn't care about other people's feelings. Didn't they have any humanity left? Was human life so little in their eyes? Life after his death was very difficult. He was the only one who could have saved me from the events that I suffered afterward. My savior was gone!

Chapter 2

Whistling Past the Graveyard

At the blueness of the skies and in the warmth of summer,
we remember them.
—Sylvan Kamens and Rabbi Jack Reimer

I was too numb to my father's death; I do not remember how my mother handled everything. What I know is how strong she was that she wiped our tears while hiding hers. Initially, we as a family couldn't acknowledge that Dad had left us. I used to think he was someplace far, far away, yet not gone for eternity. I would even see him in my thoughts and dreams and search for him after waking up.

It took many days and weeks to realize that my father was not returning, that our lives had to be deprived of him forever, and that he would not be a part of events we planned together for the future. This was the moment that knocked me in an unexpected way.

Even though my mother was also grieving, she put on a brave face and consoled us. She didn't let us know how much she was suffering. My mother did not only lose her husband but her best friend, her soulmate, and her biggest support.

Unaware of what was happening around me, I suffered in silence. I suffered, but everything seemed far away. It was as if I weren't myself . . . as if it were happening to someone else and I were watching from the sidelines.

My mother had to take on the role of my father. She worked hard only to make our life easy and peaceful. It wasn't easy for us, especially in this society where you could come across predators on every step, but Mom prevailed.

I sometimes understood my mother, and sometimes I didn't. I didn't know what all this meant. My mind was on a thin string where one step wrong would make it distressed. All I knew was that nothing would be the same again. Our life had now completely changed, no matter how many times we denied it. We had lost our most important, most precious person.

Not having my father there to be a part of my achievements and failures and not being able to venture the stones of my existence with him was an idea inconceivable to me. The size of the circumstance sank in once I started to go back to reality. Every one of the trivial issues that I used to stress over, all that had directed my life, appeared to be so immaterial now.

On occasion, I didn't have a clue how to move in my life. I tried to get myself together, not for me but for my family—my mother and siblings. My soul continued to float off to daydreams about my father, concerning the amount I missed him and the times when I had really wanted him to be there with me.

The change came when I quit contemplating what I needed my life to be and started thinking about what it really had become. I had to acknowledge my conditions and continue on with my life on the grounds that the world was not going to pause and sit tight for me.

One significant change that came after my father had left us was caring about my mother's well-being. Subsequent to losing a father, I got additionally wary of her well-being and prosperity. The smallest unsettling influence on her well-being caused dread and tension. Also, the most difficult aspect was causing her to comprehend the reason why I was being distrustful with regard to it.

My mother started working a few months later. Being the eldest sibling, I took care of my younger brothers. When my mother was busy, I took care of them like a mother. I took that role too seriously. I guess that was how a young girl would realize her responsibility.

It wasn't easy in the beginning. When I began to cook, I experienced getting burned, burning food, and wasting ingredients. I got exhausted and sometimes frustrated, running around the house to do errands. I remember an incident when I completely broke down physically, mentally, and emotionally.

The first time I cooked, I made risotto for my family. It wasn't easy for me, but I wanted to put a smile on my loved ones' faces, so I took the challenge. After the first try went well, I started cooking it almost every day for my siblings.

One day, my mother came back from home exhausted as she did two jobs.

My brother started crying and told her, "I can no longer eat risotto!"

"What happened?" my mother asked, surprised and worried. She turned toward me and said, "Why is he crying?"

"I think it's my fault," I said, lowering my head. "It wasn't good enough."

"Child, what are you talking about?" She lifted my head and looked me in the eye. "What is wrong? What is not good enough? And why do you think it is your fault?"

"H-he wanted to eat risotto, and because you were not there, I cooked it for him, b-but I guess it was not good," I cried. "I am sorry, Mother, I made him sad. I could not look after my siblings, it is my fault."

"No, child, it isn't," she said and wrapped me in her arms. Patting my back, she said, "You did your best, it's okay if it wasn't good this time. It happens most of the time. Sometimes, I also fail, so don't worry and keep trying hard."

My mother's advice made me work harder, and without breaking a sweat, I was able to make the best risotto for my brother. Seeing him smile, I realized the burns that I got from the fire and the cuts were worth it.

We did not have disposable diapers in those times; we used to take cotton ones that were washable for reuse. It became troublesome for me as I had no idea how to fix or change diapers. Because I did not want to burden my mother with home chores and the responsibilities of my siblings, I learned how to change diapers.

Everything changed in just a few months. A once-carefree girl was bound to be trapped in a tight circle. I could no longer play with my friends. They invited me, but I always declined as I had to look after my siblings.

I could never return to who I used to be when my father was with me. Having been through many failures and meltdowns, I finally learned to cook, trying my best every time. I made a motto: "One step at a time."

My mother and I watched over the kids in shifts. When I was in school, my mother took care of them. When I came back from school, it was my turn to care for them so that our mother could go to work. I had to do my homework in a rush so as not to let my brothers feel abandoned or miss anything. However, in the midst of it, I did not let anything affect my studies.

I loved to study, and I still do! It has always been my passion to learn about new things. I got excited when I found something knowledgeable. I got straight As in all my subjects. When I lost my father, it became difficult for me to study because I had to spend all my time looking after my siblings and managing the house. So I had to study when my siblings went to sleep.

I am really grateful to my mother that she did not make me quit school due to financial problems. She endured everything silently and never showed us her pain. I could never figure out her feelings and emotions at that time, but I did know that she had lost a vital part of her life. Nevertheless, there was nothing that could stop her from being the fierce woman that she was, not even my father's passing, even though it did bring her life to a halt.

> Life is like riding a bicycle; to keep your balance,
> you must keep moving.
> —Albert Einstein

All of us helped our mother in our own capacities. My seven-year-old younger brother aided me in whatever way he could—such as folding clothes, setting the table, and also taking care of our youngest sibling. Trying to mitigate the loss of our father, our mother tried to give us everything possible for her. We had nearly everything we needed in material terms just like other children with both parents present did.

Nonetheless, losing my father was a big shortcoming. I am grateful for my neighbors who were there for us in that difficult time. They weren't obliged to, but they helped us in whatever they could. I was comforted by their warm response and hospitality. They looked after us when my mother wasn't able to or when she was at work.

My uncle and aunt also stood by us. They visited us frequently and brought groceries and snacks. They treated us like their own children and never let us feel alone and sad. My aunt was always there for me, and whatever I needed, she bought it for me. She always said, "Darling, I am always there for you. Let me know whatever you need, and I will bring it for you."

People would console us; they would say things like, "Things will go back to normal," or "Everything will be all right," and "I can feel what you are going through."

* * *

I opened my eyes and glanced around the room. *Where am I?* The room was empty; no sign of any furniture was there. It only had a big window from where some air traveled into the room. The lights were off; the only source of light was the moonlight.

Perhaps I slept while completing my homework? I don't remember when I slept. *Are the kids in bed?* I thought. I roamed my eyes around the room, trying to find out any clue as to what was going on . . .

"Child?" a sweet voice called out in the distance.

"Huh?" I gazed around the room, confused.

"Child?" the voice whispered again.

"Who is there?" I asked.

"Look at me, my child," the voice whispered again. I glanced around, pursuing the place the voice was coming from.

"Father?" I murmured, still shocked. I could not believe it; my father was there. He was alive and standing in front of me.

"Yes, my child," he smiled.

"Fa-father?" stuttering, I asked. "But . . . what . . . how?"

"Calm down . . . relax. Breathe." He moved toward me and comforted me.

"Are you alive, Father? You are with us, right? You didn't leave us!" I shouted, excited. "Where is Mother? I need to tell her. She would be so happy!"

"I am sorry, darling," my father frowned.

"Why?" I asked. "Why are you sorry, Father?"

"I am not real, darling. We are in your dream." He stared at me, guilty and apologetic.

"What! No! Please tell me it's not true," I pleaded desperately.

"I am sorry, child," he murmured again and again, "I really am sorry."

"Why? Why can't you be here with us?" I cried. "Why did you have to leave, Father?"

"It was bound to happen. I didn't want to leave you people, but I had no choice. Nobody can fight fate."

I wrapped my arms around him and laid my head on his shoulders. I had no clue how long I wept; the tears kept flowing from my eyes, not knowing how to slow down. My eyes were turning red and swollen; my father patted me and leaned back to look at me.

"Don't cry. You are my bravest child! You are strong."

"I wouldn't be anything without you, Father! I miss you . . . Mom misses you too . . . We all miss you a lot!"

"I know," he said. "Remember, my love, there are certain things in our life that can never be changed. It doesn't matter how much we want to and how hard we try to change them, they will never go back to how we want them."

"Then . . . then what should we do, Father?"

"We must accept them . . . We should not fight them and know that nothing can be done to change them," my father explained. "My child, I know you are courageous. I want you to know I am always here for you, I will never leave your side! Just close your eyes and call me."

I nodded.

"I want you to be brave and keep going in your life, to never lose hope, no matter where you are or what you have gone through. You won't lose hope, right?"

"Yes, Father, I won't."

"That's my beautiful daughter."

We remained quiet for a second, reminiscing about the moment as we knew we wouldn't get it again!

"Take care of yourself, your siblings, and your mother. I want you to be happy. I want to see you smile again." He kissed me on the forehead, smiling faintly, tears in his eyes. Slowly, he started to disappear.

"Wait . . . Father!" I extended my hand toward him, trying to grasp him, but only caught dust in return. I desperately tried to reach out for him, but the more I moved, the more he dispersed into thin air.

Gasping, I woke up from my dream.

This dream that I vaguely remember now appeared when I was younger. The aftermath of the dream involved crying rivers after I woke up. The illusion was a clear and permanent reminder that my father was not with us anymore. The dream haunted me for weeks, forbidding me to fall asleep peacefully.

* * *

There wasn't a single moment when I did not miss my father. His voice, his laugh, the wrinkles on his face when he smiled, the tender way he used to call me, the soft pat on my shoulder when he was proud of me, and his infinite love for our family—I missed and still miss all of it!

Whenever I thought about him, only one thing came into my mind: I wish we had more time with him. I wanted to show him how much I loved him. I wanted to make him proud when I received good grades or when I would have held out my degree to him. There were so many things that were left unsaid, loads of stuff to do, and countless bucket lists to fulfill.

It was hard for me to believe that he would never come back. As a kid, I prayed day and night to catch one glimpse of my father, that maybe it all was a bad joke and he would appear out of nowhere and say, "Got you."

The passing years proved to me that it was just my wishful thought and nothing else. I missed my father when there were school performances or events where fathers got involved in school activities. I had no one to help me. I sometimes felt disheartened when I saw my friends enjoying great moments with their fathers.

I couldn't even go on school trips because we barely managed our household expenses. Once, I did go on a trip to Montenegro, but my friends and teachers paid for the trip expenses.

> It's hard to watch people change, but it's even harder to
> remember who they used to be.
> —Wiz Khalifa

People I know started to view us siblings differently; they took pity on us and our situation. According to them, my mother was not good because she would leave us alone and go out to work. Gradually, many people started changing; their looks and their words kept haunting me. My body would start to shiver, and goose bumps formed on my skin; their taunting whispers and penetrating eyes made me feel small.

"Look at her! How can she dress up when her husband is no more?"

"Why do the kids need that? They don't even have their father anymore!"

"She leaves her kids at home? I wonder what kind of a mother she is!"

"Did you see that? She was smiling! How can she? Her husband is dead!"

"I cannot believe those poor kids are alone now! How will they survive without a father?"

No matter what people said, I always stood by my mother's side. I realized how she struggled to provide for us to live a better life and make it easier for us in the absence of our father.

I wanted to run away from all my problems to a place where there would be serenity. My mind and heart were in a tug of war, screaming at each other. My heart wanted to mourn for the loss and paint the world red, while my mind wanted tranquility and isolation.

On the one hand, I wanted to forget about the pain and move on, and on the other, I wanted to remain in despair. I thought that losing my father was the only thing that could go wrong in my life, but life had so many more troubles in store for me. With no clue, I was advancing to a devastating storm!

Chapter 3

War in Bosnia

The broken heart. You think you will die, but you keep living,
day after day after terrible day.
—Charles Dickens

In 1992, a war started between Bosnia and Herzegovina, which led the Serb forces to target non-Serbs. The first military actions were taken on April 8, 1992, in Foca, and Serb forces took over the entire town within ten days. By the middle of July, the villages that surrounded the town were also under attack.

The estimated population of Foca was 40,513. The ethnic groups included 51 percent Muslims, 45 percent Serbians, and 3 percent of other beliefs. The Serbs military forces, premilitary people, police officers, and Serbian villagers robbed and burned the Muslims' houses. The majority of the Muslim community was brutally beaten down and murdered, while all the survivors were imprisoned in one place.

Next, the Serbian military separated the men and the women and imprisoned all the men at Foca Kazneno-Popravni Dom, now called Foca Prison. Some men remained in prison for more than two years.

The women, the old, and the children were imprisoned in their houses, apartments, and motels. The detention venues in Foca and nearby villages included Partizan Sports Hall, Foca High School, among others. Little girls and women were forced to stay in those places in unhealthy and harrowing conditions. They were ill-treated, and they had no proper supply of food and other necessary resources.

* * *

It all started when we were still recovering from my father's passing. It had not been long since we had been mourning for him when my life started to get far worse. April 6, 1992, was supposed to be yet another day, but it turned out to be a day like never before.

As usual, I got up early in the morning and started getting ready for school. My mother, who was busy preparing something in the kitchen, called me to the living room. She sounded panicked.

"What is wrong, Mother?" I asked, running to the living room, worried sick and thinking something was wrong with my siblings or my mother had some trouble.

"Look at the news," she exclaimed. "Something is happening in a town not far from ours!"

We both silently watched the news. The news reporter was talking about an incident that happened in a nearby town.

After my father's passing, my mother and I started to get anxious about anything that would create a problem for us. It was a frightening event, and we got scared that our town could also face the same fate.

"What will happen now, Mother?" I asked her, horrified and disturbed.

"I don't know, child," she said, tense. "Do not go to school today, you should stay home today."

"But, Mother . . ."

"No! My gut feeling is telling me something is going to happen," my mother interrupted me. Her stern face showed that she was serious and would scold me if I insisted. "I am terrified right now. I don't want to lose any of you, you people are the only ones who matter to me now. Go and wake up your siblings. I am going to prepare breakfast."

"All right." I did what she told me. It was not like I did not trust my mother's instincts and decision, but the news spooked me a little. I wanted to know more about what was going on, but I knew it could be dangerous for my family and me.

The very next day, my class teacher visited us before I could leave for school. My mother and I were surprised by her sudden visit.

"The kid does not have to go to school anymore this year," she said.

"W-what do you mean?" my mother asked, shocked. "Did something happen in school? Was it something she did? I will try to . . ."

"No, no. It's not something like that," my teacher said and smiled. "Do not worry, she hasn't done anything wrong!" She frowned, upset.

"Because of the recent events in the town, it was decided that we would end the school year. All the students are being promoted to the next year."

We were speechless. My mother's instinct was correct; something had gone wrong!

"Here is your report card." The teacher handed me my report card. "I wish you the best for the coming years. I hope you excel in your studies."

Although distressed, I was a little happy that the school year ended earlier. I did not have to work two ways now; I could easily look after my siblings without worrying about my studies. I was relaxed that my life would be easy from now on, and I could finally enjoy things.

I was ecstatic, not realizing what the chaos was brewing for all of us!

Two days after the news, on April 8, 1992, the Serbs started to gather in groups, and they looked at us strangely. There was hidden meaning in their eyes. Chills went down my back whenever I had to pass by them. Nobody knew what was going through their minds.

The same day, they started setting up barricades at every entry and exit in the city, which made it difficult for us to even move within the city. The neighbors started getting troubled, not knowing what was going on in the city. The smoldering eyes and the whispers were all we knew; it was confirmed that a storm was coming that would destroy everything.

My mother, who was already anxious from all the chaos, came to me one day and said, "Pack your bags, we have to leave the place right now."

"But where are we going, Mother?"

"There is a nearby village, my friend lives there. We are going there for a few days."

"But why should we leave our house? What will happen to our house then?"

"We will come back when everything calms down, but right now, we don't have any other choice. If we stay here, I am afraid something will go wrong."

"Do you promise, Mother?"

"I promise. When everything settles down, we will be back," she said, kissing my forehead fondly.

I could understand my mother's fear. After all, she was a woman who had lost her loving husband, so she could not afford to lose her children. It was not easy for us to leave our house, as all the siblings had been born and bred there. It was the first time we were leaving the house without any clue when we would be back.

It was such a wishful thought that everything would be back to normal in a few days. No one in Foca knew that nothing would return to normal for the next five years. It was peaceful for a few days; we settled into our new environment, but it did not last long. One day, the Serbs entered the village and threatened the people:

"We know many of you who have left your houses and are hiding over here. Return to your houses right now! If you fail to return to your house, we will take everything from you. This is your last chance. Don't blame us then!"

The threat scared us all. Since none of us wanted to lose our properties, we all went back to our respective houses. However, my mother asked me to stay in the village and promised me that she would come back in a few weeks. After they left, I was all right for some days. I did not want to disobey my mother, so I tried as hard as possible to stay there.

Eventually, I got homesick. Actually, this was the first time I had been away from my siblings and mother for so long. Since I missed my family immensely, I returned home before she could come for me. I was so foolish to think that everything would be better after I got home. I didn't know the calm was just a whirlwind, and I was unaware of what was awaiting me at home.

My family was already under house arrest by the time I reached the city. We were forbidden to go out of the house. The only place they allowed us to go was in front of the building in the daytime. The Serb military forces had taken complete control of the city. They overpowered us and asked us to do whatever they wanted. It was the most disturbing time for everyone in the city.

Every day they imposed an all-night curfew for all people, even for the Serb residents; it was only the Serb army that roamed the streets. I was afraid of closing my eyes, wondering what might happen if I closed them for even a few seconds. I missed my father so badly at that time. I had a feeling if he had been there, I would have never felt so unsafe.

The Serb forces cut down the power and any means of food sources. The food we had in the freezer had gone stale and finished eventually. The forces did not allow us to go out and buy food; we were forced to starve in our houses and our own hometown.

The Serb army targeted the Bosnian Muslims. They separated our family members, putting both genders in different places. The women and children were put in residential and public locations, and the men were taken to the camps. Along with several other women, I was kept in an apartment, and we shared whatever food was available.

> In matters of style, swim with the current; in matters of
> principle, stand like a rock.
> —Thomas Jefferson

When the war started, I was in house imprisonment with my mom and brothers in our apartment for five months with no supply of power and food. Those five months were tormenting for us. The Serb forces were always keeping an eye on us; we could not do anything without asking them.

My siblings used to cry of hunger; they didn't know the problem we were stuck in. My mother was mentally disturbed because of the imprisonment and that there was no food and power. In fact, she felt guilty that she was unable to provide for us, but it was not her fault. My whole family was helpless, just like others.

The Serb forces were so cruel that if they found any local Serbians helping Bosnian Muslims, they would even kill those people. They did not want anyone to help the Bosnian Muslims, not even their own kin. They had a deep hatred toward us; they wanted us to leave, wanting the place for themselves only.

Luckily, we had a good neighborhood. My family was friends with Serb people who lived in our apartment building. They helped us and provided us with food secretly. They were all afraid of helping us, but their kind heart didn't stop them from caring for us.

My father had a good Serbian friend. He tried his level best to help us; he and his wife would risk their lives to visit us during the curfew at night. The humble couple would deliver food to us through the window. We were grateful for their courage, kindness, and generosity.

My mother also had a good Serbian friend who lived next door. He felt pity for us. He used to put food in his house and give the key to my mom to fetch food from his house at night.

Along with the Serbian military forces, some local Serbians also started discriminating against the Muslims. Many of the neighbors and friends distanced themselves from us; some did so because they developed hatred, while some just wanted to keep their families safe.

I was disappointed with their behavior. I thought they would fight for us and stay with us forever. The military forces influenced their perspectives, breaking the bond we had with them. People would set houses on fire just for their entertainment; they also slaughtered boys and men without caring about anything.

We, the Muslim community, hoped that everything was a misunderstanding and it would be resolved soon. The reality hit us hard when we began to realize that it would never be the same again as days passed. We had lost everything: our safety, our mental health, the people we loved, the healthy environment in the city, the place we once considered our home, and the peace. It was like we were living in a different state or getting abandoned by our loved ones.

There was a couple of apartments in our building where Muslim families lived. They also thought that our neighbors would not go against us at any cost. But we were wrong; we all were living among people who had turned into monsters in a blink of an eye.

The whole community made an error in assuming that people would not betray them for their good. It is human nature to consider things that are beneficial to them rather than others.

During the day, the Muslim community would stay in their apartments and gather in one apartment at night; we used the basement to get to that one place. Those women would then sleep in one place, as it was easier for us, and for some reason, we felt safer when we were together.

Every woman was going through the same thing; we could understand each other's emotions and feelings. We knew that we only had each other during that difficult time. The mothers used to get afraid for their daughters, for their purity and their innocent minds. However, peace in the city and peace of mind were not for us anymore.

Some days later, the Serb forces started taking young girls to detention camps, apartments, and motels. It was a nightmare for the girls and their mothers; they cried and begged the Serb forces to let their daughters go but to no avail. No one could stop them!

Every day my mother and I would hear women screaming for their daughters. They did not care if the girl was young or adult; they would part them from their families. In fact, many of the girls the Serbs picked had dolls in their tiny hands.

It was horrifying for me and more for my mother as she dreaded for me being the next victim. She would jump every time anyone tried to approach her and would instantly hide me in her arms, frightened and tense. When my father's Serbian friend realized what was happening, he took me to his apartment for my safety. He was a loyal friend to my father; he never wanted his friend's daughter to go through something so gruesome.

When the Serb forces found out that I was with his family, they started threatening him. They asked him to hand me over or face the same fate as the Muslims.

Since he had a wife and three children, for his family's safety, he had no other choice but to let me go back. He was sorry that he could not save me. I understood that he was powerless in front of the military forces. So he let me go back home to ensure his own family would not have problems because of me.

As time went on, people started to behave more brutally toward us. Gathered in one place at night, we felt safe. When we got back to the apartment in the morning, we would find the doors open.

"Who would that be, Mother?" I asked, confused.

"The Serbs visited our apartments, child," my mother said in a sorrowful voice.

As there wasn't anything that went missing or stolen, my mother soon realized they were going there for me.

"I am afraid, Mother," I cried out one day. "I am really scared. Where are they taking the girls? Will they also take me? What will they do to me?" My innocent questions would torment my mother.

She could not tell her daughter what was going on. How could she? No mother would want her daughter to experience that.

One day, my mother's best friend came to the apartment and took everything she liked.

"What are you doing? Why are you taking my things?" my mother shouted at her.

"I am taking all the things you have in this apartment."

"Why? Why are you doing all this?"

"Don't you know? It is my right to take everything I want! You won't need this anymore, you don't have the right to have them," she replied bitterly.

We were upset about how people could change so suddenly. The war was a terrible event!

* * *

It was all a frightening nightmare for me and for all of us—something that I had to endure without any complaint. Even if I tried to shout out to the world to ask them and complain about my sufferings, nobody would know the answer!

I always questioned myself about the incidents that happened at the time.

What is the reason behind all that misconduct?

Why are they doing all of that to us?

What thought made them go this far?

What did I even do to deserve this?

Am I really this unfortunate?

I, to this day, have not found the answers to these questions. I wonder how one human being could treat the other this way; did they never hear our cries and pain?

> You have to understand that people have to pay the price for
> peace. If you dare to struggle, you dare to win.
> —Fred Hampton

Chapter 4

Chained in Thorns

Although the life of a person is in a land full of thorns and
weeds, there is always a space in which the good seed can grow.
You have to trust God.
—Pope Francis

The Serbs' abuse went on for months; nobody cared about how we
were treated. The Muslim community was mentally and emotionally
disturbed by their behaviors. The woman thought they were at least safe
with their daughters and that nothing could harm them if they were all
together, but they didn't know what the Serb soldiers had planned for them
was far worse!

A parent never wants their children to go through hardships, let alone
one that is beyond their control. I was a kid at that time, not knowing what
was going on, but my mother had an instinct; she would look at my face
and continuously cry.

"My child, always remember," she would say and hug me tightly,
weeping silently, "no matter what happens in the future, remember that
your brothers and I love you. Your father will always love you. It isn't your
fault, darling."

"What is going on, Mom?" I would ask her innocently, but she never
replied to my questions. Instead, her cries would get louder.

I could just simply gaze at my mother; she would remain quiet, praying
that someone would protect us. I was young enough not to understand my
mother's troubles.

I remember once when all the women were sleeping in the big room,
a loud sound was heard by someone in the neighborhood. Startled from

our sleep, we all huddled up together and glanced around, trying to find a clue as to what was going on.

Thud!

We heard the loud voice again, but this time we were able to understand that it was coming from outside. One woman mustered up the courage and slowly moved toward the small hole that allowed us to see outside but wasn't big enough for the Serbs to spot us.

"No . . . Mom, where are you going?" Her daughter clenched her arm, stopping her mother from moving forward.

"Don't worry, nothing will happen to me," she said, soothing her daughter. "Wait for a second, I am just over."

Moving away from her daughter, the woman trudged forward and silently looked out the hole. A minute had gone by when she suddenly gasped and moved back in horror. The woman's eyes widened in fear, her hands and mouth trembling.

"What . . . what is wrong?" her daughter asked. "Mother! What is wrong? Tell me! What did you see, Mom?"

And one by one, the woman gathered around her, asking her what she had seen. But the woman was shaken up. Nothing could be heard from her mouth other than a word that made a disgusting shiver go down our bodies.

"Blood."

* * *

I still remember the day when Miko, the commander of the police in Miljevina, and Pero, the head of Chetniks, came to get me. It came as a shock to me that my family was accustomed to these people.

My mother told me after the war ended that she knew Pero because my grandfather's father helped Pero's mother in World War II.

"What is going to happen now, Pero?" my mother asked Pero.

"I cannot tell you what exactly is going to happen or what the soldier had decided," he said.

"Please keep her safe at all costs. I don't want her to go through anything."

"Do not worry, we will put her in a safe place," they told my mother, reassuring her that no harm would come to me.

"Take care of yourself, my child." My mother clasped my hands in hers and squeezed them lightly.

"When will I come back home, Mother?" I asked.

"Soon, my child. Soon." She kissed me on my forehead.

I was taken to a house in Miljevina; it was about ten meters away from the Karaman House.

When I entered that house, I learned that a girl was already living there, who, upon recognizing her, I found out was a girl I knew. With her were her uncle, aunt, two children, and the old grandmother. I was advised to stay over there until the beginning of August.

It was a little confusing for me at first, knowing that things had turned out to be different than I had imagined. I didn't want to think of anything, and I just wanted to go back to my home.

> Society indeed conspires to keep you ball and chained.
> —Douglas Coupland

While I stayed there, the soldiers—especially Rado, Misko, Pedo, and Pero—used to visit the house. Rado was my neighbor; we lived in the same building before the war.

I would get worried whenever they visited, fearing they would mistreat us, but they behaved in a friendly way. They didn't maltreat us, and we didn't have any problems with them. I thought they might be good people and that they were different from the bad ones. Little did I know, they were the worst!

* * *

Around mid-August, we were shifted to another house without knowing the real reason behind it. The only thing I remember clearly is that we were swapped with other girls. The soldiers brought the girl and me outside to the Karman House, a place which the soldiers conspired and made into a breeding ground for assaulters and war criminals.

When we reached there, we saw Rado, Misko, Pedo, and Drago were already present there with four girls. They all were in a deep discussion. The girl and I had clasped each other's hands tightly; we were scared of what would happen to us now. I wanted to scream, but no voice would come out no matter how hard I tried.

The clock ticked slowly; it was an agonizing moment for us. We were waiting for our fate, asking ourselves what more we had to go through and when all that suffering would end. The dark, heavy clouds rained heavily and thundered, looking down upon us as if crying for our life.

After the discussion was done, they moved the four girls into the house while pushing the girl and me into the black car parked on the curb.

"Where are we going?" I asked the soldier, but he didn't reply.

"Rado!" I shouted, thinking he might save me. "Wait, that guy over there is my neighbor!"

"He won't help you, sweetie," the soldier mocked, chuckling. "He was the one who gifted you to us!"

"No, it couldn't be! Please take me back to the house. Please, I beg you!"

"Shut up! I am getting tired of your yelling! Just sit down before I slap you!"

"W-wait! No—"

"It's no use!" the girl interrupted me, halting me from slapping my hands on the window. "No one can save us from them, there is no need to try. You will fail." I could feel that she had given up and resorted to her fate.

"W-what are you talking about? Why are you not fighting with me?"

"There is no use fighting them."

"B-but still, we could try, maybe they would hear us."

The girl quieted down and turned toward the other side, looking out the window. I frowned and was about to shout again when I heard her faint voice.

"Monsters don't care about anybody. They will do what they want."

Hearing her, I backed down defeated and leaned my head on the back of the seat. Wordlessly I wept, listening to my mother's scream that resonated from the house.

I was surprised and disgusted that I knew a guy like Rado. Even though he never sexually assaulted me, he was the worst in my eyes as he was the one who handed me over to other soldiers in exchange for some other girl.

How could he exchange girls for his own pleasure—and that too, a minor! Doesn't he have his own kids, his family? Doesn't he have any kindness left? I thought.

Rado, Pero, Miko, Drago, and Gojo were the owners of everything they wanted—the masters of life and death. They thought they were gods and could rule over anything, animal or human!

Drago drove us to the town that was named Trnovaca. The bumpy ride was quiet. Every one of us lost in our thoughts, where two people were anxious about the unseen future in contrast to the other two who were pleased that they destroyed the lives of little girls.

I felt numb and monotonous, recalling every memory of my beloved father and imagining how he would have saved me if only he had been there. I imagined my mother's smiling face, the twinkle in her eyes, and how the wrinkles appeared on her face whenever she was in deep thought. I recalled when she used to run around us siblings, trying to feed us. The love and affection would be visible in her eyes.

I thought about my two little brothers' antics and mischievousness and the way they used to giggle when the prank they pulled on me was successful. Oh, how they pretended to be upset and sad when I scolded them.

The whole night passed in anticipation, thinking about what these people would do to us. Hana beside me wept silently, her head in her hands. I knew it was painful for her, but I didn't know how I should comfort her. Placing my hand on her shoulder, I caressed her arm. Hana glanced up at me.

"Don't c-cry," I stammered, teary-eyed. "Things will be better soon."

"No," Hana shook her head. "Nothing will be better now. You don't know anything that they are doing."

"What are you talking about?"

"They will destroy us just like they had every other girl in my neighborhood. We are not safe now."

I moved her head to my shoulder and embraced her in my arms, trying to soothe her. Throughout the ride, Hana kept mumbling, "We are not safe," until she finally dozed off into a deep slumber.

I stared out at the blurring trees and smiled when I saw the moon in the sky shining on us. *At least someone is with us!* I didn't know when and how, but I slowly succumbed to sleep, calling for my father.

"Father, you are closer to God now," I mumbled, clenching my hand tightly. "Please ask him to save me from this hell."

* * *

"Wake up!" Someone was shaking me continuously. "Don't you hear, girl? Wake up!"

I immediately woke up from my slumber, hearing the deep, angry voice. The unnamed soldier was standing in front of me, his face furious. Turning toward Hana, he woke her up and dragged her out of the car violently.

"You both have taken enough of my time!" he shouted. "Go inside the house now!"

Stumbling, Hana and I walked toward the house. The soldier kept pushing us to move while Drago followed behind us. In the living room, we found three more girls there, along with Gojo, who was sitting on the couch.

"Who are these girls?" he asked the soldier, staring at us from head to toe. A shiver went down my body, disgusted by the hunger in his eyes.

"Sir, the girls are from Miljevina," the soldier standing beside Drago told him.

"Are they from Pero?" Gojo asked. "Did that guy send them?"

"Yes, sir!" the soldier confirmed. "What should we do with them?"

"Send them back. I don't want to have anything to do with Pero," he remarked heatedly.

"But—"

The soldier was silenced when Gojo stared at him sharply. He knew better than to fight with the devil; obeying his command was the only way to stay out of his rage. The soldier quietly whispered, "Okay," and along with Drago, he took us out of the house.

"Where do we take them now, Drago?" the soldier asked, motioning us to sit in the car.

"I don't know," he answered. "Let us leave them in an apartment in Brod for now."

And that they did. The house in Brod was where my life was ruined for the worst . . . like a ship that was sinking in the deep, hollow ocean.

There is only one prospect worse than being chained to an intolerable existence: The nightmare of a botched attempt to end it.
—Arthur Koestler

Chapter 5

Predators of Hell

I'd rather not have to come face to face with predators.
I'd rather not be harassed. But no.
Those weren't my choices to make, were they?
—Chinmayi

The emotions I was going through on that day are not something I want to experience again. Not now, not ever! It was all so suffocating for me.

I felt like what you feel walking along a dark, empty road, without any streetlamp to guide you, not knowing where the road would end or what you may encounter ahead. In moments like those, you are terrified and distressed that something or someone would appear out of nowhere. That was what I felt. That was what went through my mind that day, and my eyes were moving back and forth with terror, trying to find an escape route.

I didn't know where we were going, nor did I want to know, as my instincts told me it was something beyond evil!

* * *

The car ride was a long one; it was filled with anticipation and fear. Nobody uttered a single word as if we all had gone mute. The occasional sniffling and whimpering were the only sounds that could be heard.

Wrapping our arms around each other, the girl and I tried to find comfort in each other. The little squeeze of our joined hands would somehow comfort us for a second, but the devilish grin of those monsters sitting in the front would dampen it the very next second.

"We are here!" the soldier shouted when Drago shut down the car engine. "Come on out, you girls! We don't have the whole day!"

They fiercely pushed us out of the cars and forced us to walk inside the house. As it was dark, I didn't know where or what was around the house, just that it was a lonely abandoned house.

"Hey!" Drago called out. "Veso? Are you there?"

"What is it?" a man asked, walking out from the living room. Behind him was another guy. "Who are those girls?"

"You and Pusa are going to take care of them till we decide what to do with them," Drago told them.

The soldier pushed the girl and me into a room while the men talked in the hall. The girl was crying hysterically, clenching my dress in her hands. I could only console her at that time as I myself did not know what was going on.

We heard a loud slam and loud voices coming from the hall. It seemed like Veso did not like the idea of having us there either.

"What is going on, Pusa?" he yelled. "Why are they here? What are we going to do with them?"

"I don't know," Pusa answered indifferently. "Do whatever you want with them. No one is going to stop you, Veso."

A cold shiver went down my spine; Pusa's words disgusted me. It made me want to puke again and again until there wasn't anything left in me!

"I don't want them to stay here." Then Veso's voice quieted down. The rest of the conversation continued in low whispers.

Pusa and Veso left us in that room alone, making us sigh in relief. They let us think that maybe we would be all right. It was daytime; we both were exhausted but didn't want to close our eyes in case something might happen.

I knew I couldn't sleep, not in a devastating condition. I was fully alert, and my father's words echoed in my mind: "Never let your guard down, my child," he had said one day, stroking my hair. "No matter where you are, be conscious of your surroundings. We never know from where the demons will come!"

Oh, Father, if only you were here . . . , I thought, sighing.

Glancing toward the girl, I noticed how sleep-deprived she was. Her eyes had gone red due to lack of sleep; her eyelids kept shutting down, but she would forcefully open them again.

"You should sleep," I said to her.

"Huh?" she said, confused. "B-but what about you? Don't you also want to sleep?"

"It's okay," I told her. "I don't want to sleep."

She stared at me, doubtful.

"All right, how about we nap and guard in shifts?" I suggested. "Right now, I will guard you, and you take a nap. And when you wake up, you can guard me, and I will take a nap. How about this?"

"Sounds good to me, I guess."

I exhaled, happy that she was not resisting it. The girl lay her head on my lap and went into a deep slumber the moment she closed her eyes.

It went quiet after that. She slept, leaving me alone in the dark room to reminisce about everything. I felt like I was trapped in a small box that was heavily shut down, halting my escape. It was all about waiting and waiting for the unexpected.

After some hours, the girl woke up and asked me to take a nap. I reluctantly did what I was asked as my sibling instinct wanted me to protect her as my own. I don't remember how long I slept; it was already nighttime when I was woken up by a chilling scream. Shakily, I glanced around my surroundings, trying to locate the cause behind the scream.

My eyes widened when I saw someone lying down on the sofa beside the bed. I squinted my eyes in the dark to figure out who it was and was surprised to find it was Veso. Panicked, I turned beside myself to warn the girl but was startled to see the space empty.

Where did she go? I thought. Did they—

Another scream halted my thoughts. It was then that I realized the screams were coming from her. My breathing hitched, and my mouth went dry, making it hard for me to swallow.

"Wh-where i-is the girl?" I asked in the dark room.

"With Pusa," Veso replied quietly.

"Wha-what is going on? Wh-what is happening to her?" I asked him.

"Nothing," he replied. "It's nothing you should get yourself concerned about."

"C-can't you help her?" I asked desperately. "Please help her!"

Silence fell in the room. I waited for him to reply, but he didn't. Resigned, I leaned my head on the wall and silently wept, listening to the poor girl's wails. Her forlorn shouts for help made my hair stand, and my body shuddered in horror.

I didn't know what was happening to her at that time, and how would I? I was only sixteen at that time.

"I can't," Veso gently said. "I couldn't."

* * *

I couldn't sleep that night, despite the understanding that Veso had no intention of mistreating me. I didn't close my eyes for a second. I was thankful that he left me alone the whole night.

The next day, we were shifted to another location; this time, they took us to an apartment. My hell started there in that house at Brod.

Veso and Pusa left us there with other soldiers. Two girls were already there when we entered the apartment, huddled up in a corner beside the sofa. The soldiers pushed the girl and me toward the other girls.

Within a few minutes, the atmosphere became heavy as soon as the soldiers piled up in the living room. Some of them were standing while some were sitting, but the common thing about them was that they were gazing at us in a disgusting way. There was hunger in each of their eyes. Gica asked the other soldiers to pick the girl they wanted; it prompted them to become more eager.

I couldn't imagine what I was hearing. I pinched myself to wake up from this nightmare but to no avail. It was the harsh reality that I wanted to avoid!

In the midst of all the chaos, the door creaked open, and a set of soldiers entered the apartment. They were covered in dirt and blood, their faces hardened. Gica joyously beckoned the soldiers to him.

"Hey!" Gica shouted. "Come over here!"

"What is it?" a guy asked.

"Raso!" he said, excited. "The very guy I was looking for! Come over here, boy, and choose the girl you want!"

Raso roamed his eyes on us, gazing at us from head to toe with his indecent eyes. I lowered my eyes as soon as he shifted his gaze to me, wanting to avoid him at all costs.

"Her," Raso declared. "I want her."

I sucked in a breath, petrified to see that his fingers were pointing toward me! I froze in my spot.

I closed my eyes tightly and clenched my hands in a fist. I heard someone walking toward us and cowered back. A hand grabbed my left shoulder and forcefully pulled me up.

"Stand up!"

"No!" I shouted. "Help me!" I extended my hands toward the other girls, asking for their help, but they all just looked at me in pity and lowered their heads.

I understood then that no one was going to save us over here. We were all doomed to go through what was to come. But I didn't want to give up, at least not this soon!

Raso dragged me to an apartment next door to Gica's. The whole way, I kept on screaming and kicking for him to let me go. I didn't know what I was fighting this hard against, but the dreadful feeling in my heart was telling me it was something aggrieved.

Do you know that feeling where you want to do anything that is in your power to stop something, but you don't know what it is? That was what I was going through on that dreadful day when they murdered my soul! It was an agonizing night for me where my dreams were silenced and my happiness was slaughtered in broad daylight.

There was suffocation in the room, as if someone had tightly wrapped their hands around my neck, choking me. My throat went dry from the constant screaming and shouting. I felt sharp needles pricking every part of my body, making my skin crawl.

There was no use! There wasn't any use. The kicks and punches did nothing to stop that monster. Instead, I only got punched in retaliation. I thought it was over, that life was over. I sank and disappeared inside myself.

The worst part was that I had my period on that day, and the stomachache worsened. Still, it didn't stop that man from ruining me! But how would it? Devils don't have humanity.

The pain was unbearable for me; I couldn't hold on to it any longer and fainted. I thought of that as transporting myself to a safe haven, to a place where my family was. I dreamed about my family, laughing and playing in a clearing. My siblings and I were running around the beautiful colored flowers and the lush, green grass. Our parents were leaning into each other's arms, smiling widely, watching us play peacefully.

But the dream didn't last long; my family started to vanish in thin air, taking my smile with them and letting me face the horrible world.

* * *

My interlocutors and hundreds of other women in other houses and apartments in Foča, Miljevina, Trnovača, and almost all surrounding places were all slaves. The creatures who called themselves soldiers and Serb people abused them daily in all forms—animals.

The life of a carefree sixteen-year-old girl was extinguished in a house on Brod, and the struggle for survival of a girl who had been captured just because of her name began.

A few days later, after that night, Veso and another younger boy took the girl and me out of the house and to a weekend cottage. They told us that they wanted to help us and were fair to us. They didn't lift a single hand on us, and we thought we were saved.

We were only there for a few hours when Gojo came to fetch us. As there was no electricity or water in that house, it was inconvenient to stay there. Seeing those conditions, Gojo said, "You people should come to my home. There are enough resources over there, you could take a bath as well and get some rest."

We had to return to Trnovace. Veso and the other guy who was guarding us came along and looked after us in that house. It was all peaceful for a few days; nobody touched us until the day our guardians were taken away from us.

The following evening, when we were all sitting in the house, Drago came into the room and stared hard at each of us. His expression told me that he wasn't happy with how things were going.

"Come outside!" he said, motioning to Veso and the younger guy. "I need to talk to you both!"

Reassuring us that no harm would come to us, the guys left with Drago. We waited hours for their return, fearing for our lives. In the end, only Drago came back without them.

Feeling uneasy about the sudden change, I asked, "Where is Veso?"

"He is gone! He is never coming back here again."

"Why?" I asked, scared.

Drago didn't reply to me and just stared at me, his expression hard. After he was satisfied with my frightened expression, he told me, "It's none of your business! Did you hear me, girl? What I do and don't do is none of your business! I decide who stays here and who doesn't, you are not in a position to question me!" He shouted violently, frightening me, "You need to understand that it is a war field! No love or relationship is allowed over here!"

Veso, the guy who was guarding me, had to obey the order. I later found out that he had been killed. I prayed for his soul to find peace. Veso, without a last name, was a hero who tried to protect innocent girls.

Chapter 6

The Gaslighting Wolves

Though her soul requires seeing, the culture around her
requires sightlessness. Though her soul wishes to speak its
truth, she is pressured to be silent.
—Clarissa Pinkola Estes,
Women Who Run with the Wolves

The nightmare wasn't over; no, it was far from over. It got worse as more time passed. There was no end to my miseries and tears; it was as if someone had sprinkled salt on my wounds. It was impossible to breathe. But why did we go through such hardships? What was the purpose behind the pain? I always used to ask questions.

The people who imprisoned me in shackles didn't only ruin young girls' lives but also made them question their self-worth. They tarnished their dignity to no end, taking joy in their suffering. As if they were gods, they ruled everything and did what they wanted—not killing us once but again and again and in the most brutal, disgusting way.

* * *

After the savior protecting us was killed, things started to go downhill, both for the other girls who were there with me and myself. One of them was a fourteen-year-old while the other three were eighteen-year-olds. All the girls used to huddle around each other, finding comfort and peace that was far away from their life.

The only soldiers who were permanently at the house were Gojo, Drago, and Gaga. Other soldiers would go in and out all day and night, but they stayed with us and made life unbearable.

During the day, the soldiers would gather us in one place, or sometimes they would even make us do chores for them, such as cooking, doing dishes, or bathing them. Whenever any one of us refused to do what they wanted, all hell would break loose.

"What the hell are you doing?" a soldier shouted at Sara once. She had mistakenly dropped a bowl, shattering it into small pieces. "Didn't I tell you what will happen to you if you break anything?"

"I . . . I . . ." Sara was at a loss for words.

"Come with me, you wench!" The soldier dragged her out of the kitchen to somewhere we didn't know, nor could we ask them.

The next time we saw Sara, her face was swollen, the corner of her lips was cut, and her eyes were empty. We knew better than to ask her what was wrong, so we remained silent and went on with our work.

In the darkness, they would come for us, gazing at us with eyes that would make anyone feel dirty and vulnerable. They would analyze the girls like how a predator analyzed his prey. It would make my skin crawl every time they looked at us with hungry eyes. And when they got interested in any girl, they would take her with them. You know that feeling when you go to a buffet and see some people looking at the many dishes for the first time, and how they jump on the first dish they see as if they have been starved for days? That was what I felt whenever I looked at the soldiers behaving like that.

Before, I couldn't understand the meaning of their glares. I always used to think they were glaring at us but in a twisted way because there was always a smile on their face. Why would they smile when they were looking at us with hatred? Oh, how naive I was, unable to grasp the real message behind those eyes; but after the experience at the house at Brod, I could comprehend it.

I remember a vague memory when one day all the girls were gathered in a room, terrified and anxious. We kept glancing at each other, nervous about our unknown fate.

"What is going to happen now? When will we go back to our home?" Hana asked innocently.

"I don't know," Sara mumbled. "I don't know anymore."

"I have lost all hope. I don't even know if I will be able to survive all this," Lejla muttered sadly.

"We couldn't lose hope right now," I said. "Our families are waiting for us! We can fight with them."

Sara and Lejla glanced at each other.

And then Sara said, "You haven't gone through what we have faced up till now. We were also like you when we got here, we wanted to fight and protect ourselves, and we did."

"But there was no use," Lejla completed Sara's words. "They still ruined us. They don't care about our feelings, they just want to crush our souls."

"Is there really no way?" Hana inquired with tears in her eyes.

"I don't think so," Sara murmured slowly.

* * *

For three weeks, Gojo, Drago, and Gaga remained with us, and after that, they were joined by a woman, Jadra, and a man, Zoki. Some of the soldiers would usually wear their uniforms while some would be in casual clothes.

When Jadra arrived at the house the first time, she was wearing her uniform, but after that, I don't think I ever saw her wear that uniform again.

One day, it happened again. First, Drago came and took a girl with him. She fought against him, kicking and screaming to let her go. We all knew what would happen to her, knowing that we would be the next victim of the vicious wolves.

"Please, not me, please," I mumbled lowly to myself. "I don't want to experience that horrible thing again. I will be a good child and will obey my mother, doing whatever she wants from me. Please, let it be a peaceful night and not an aching one!" My hands were fisted tightly, making them pale from the lack of blood flow. I had closed my eyes shut, clenching them, wanting to hide from feral eyes.

Minutes later, after Drago exited, Gojo came and took a girl with him. Now only Hana and I were left in that room. We both knew only one of us would survive the night while the other had to be slaughtered again. Hana, who was sitting on the couch, came and sat beside me, holding my hand tightly. The door creaked, and I closed my eyes, trapping myself in darkness.

"Come," Gaga said loudly. Braving myself, I opened my eyes, only to find that he was looking at Hana. Quivering, Hana stood up and slowly made her way to him. A sigh left my mouth in relief. I lowered my head, avoiding looking at Hana's helpless eyes, knowing I couldn't help her.

"Didn't you hear me?" Gaga shouted, startling me. Instantly, I glanced upward to see what was wrong and froze when I saw his eyes were already glaring at me. "Stand up, what are you waiting for?"

It was then that I realized we both wouldn't be having a peaceful night. We were doomed.

"Hurry up!"

I was trembling. My legs were numb, making it difficult for me to move forward. I forced myself to follow them as I didn't want to decorate my body with more scars than it already had. Gaga showed us into a room, slamming the door shut after he got inside.

"You people should be lucky I got you. I am not too violent, you see." He chuckled darkly. "You see, I was with Asja the previous night, and now I would be with the two of you."

Gaga tortured us, not physically but emotionally, humiliating and mocking us. He had a devilish smile on his face that showed me how pleasant it was for him to crush people who were weaker than him. What did he get from doing that? Didn't he have any remorse or guilt inside him? Was his heart dead?

After crushing our pride and self-respect, he told us, "You can go now."

What a relief! I had thought. *Maybe we are going to be safe?* My head was lowered, so I couldn't see his expression.

I turned to exit the room when he said, "Not you." Glancing up, I saw him looking in my direction. "You are going to stay with me." He turned toward Hana and motioned her to leave the room.

"What? B-but—"

"Shut up! I didn't ask for your opinion!"

"I am sorry," Hana whispered to me, her eyes ashamed, and she ran past me.

Her agony was shortened, but mine was prolonged.

I was stuck, frozen. I didn't want to go through it again. Why me? Why? What did I do wrong? Why was God punishing me like this? So many questions with no answer. Gaga started moving toward me; his prying eyes made me feel dirty. I wanted to cut off every body part that he was looking at. But I couldn't show him I was weak. No! I would fight back; I would protect myself.

As soon as he was in close proximity, I jumped up and clawed his face, digging my nails deeper into his skin, drawing blood. He was screaming to let go, but I was lost in my rage. The only mistake I made was underestimating Gaga. I thought he would leave me alone if I fought back, but he didn't! Instead, he was way worse than Raso. He shoved me to the floor with his hand on my neck, choking me tightly.

"Listen here, bitch!" he shouted. "You have two options. We could do this either my way or your way. I don't mind going your way, but I don't think you want to be dead before you see your mother again, do you?"

His cruel grasp suffocated me, and I couldn't breathe. Gaga's eyes were wide; a chill went through me when I saw how dark it was. It terrified me to no end to think how crazy his eyes looked on that day. I did not doubt that he would kill me; I knew he could. He had murdered thousands of people already, so why would he hesitate to kill a teenage girl who was only a plaything?

Slowly, I released his hair and stopped digging my nails into his shoulder. I left myself numb and retreated, giving up, letting myself go numb as if I had no soul left in me. What was I even supposed to do? I didn't want to be beaten and bruised. That night turned out to be the hardest night of my life. I was battered only to boost someone's ego, their pride.

After massacring my soul, Gaga removed himself from me and moved to the bed. His eyes were still on me, but this time he had a smug expression on his face. I couldn't understand how easy it was for people to smile after brutally destroying another person. Didn't they fear God? Did they lose their humanity? No one knew, or no one wanted to answer the obvious!

I tried to move, wanting to run away from the room, far away from him. But his voice halted my movements.

"Where are you going?"

"T-t-to the r-r-room . . . ," I stammered, avoiding his eyes.

"No, you are not. I told you already, you are staying with me." He growled.

"B-b-but please."

"No!" He glared at me. "Do you want me to beat you black and blue again?"

"N-no, I d-don't."

"Then come here and lie down. I don't want to hear any more of this."

I had now become used to sleepless nights. I couldn't sleep; I just lay there and thought about when I was free and had dreams that I wanted to accomplish. Back then, I was a carefree girl who loved and cherished her life, whose laugh was so contagious that it brought a smile to others' faces.

Where did that girl go? She was still there but not alive, breathing but not living.

I had always loved colors, amazed by the fact that they could turn a simple picture into a beautiful one: how a splash of colors could brighten anyone's life. But now I couldn't think of them, as if they had turned away from me, leaving me to drown in a dull and shattered life.

Gaga didn't let me go in the morning; he was being aggressive toward me and acting like I was his property. He showed me that some people could be so revolting that talking to them or being in their mere presence could harm anyone. Even the devil too! He continued to damage my soul, leaving scars on me that couldn't be removed or repaired again.

* * *

The next day, all the soldiers stayed in the house, assigning the girls chores. Torturing us was fun for them, and Jadra was the worst woman I had ever encountered. To date, I haven't seen a person as wicked as she was. There was a different type of rage in her eyes, as if she had a motto behind her actions.

Once, she was drunk and in a bad mood; she saw the girls and me sitting in the living area. She came marching toward us as if she had an agenda. Her eyes were glowing; the soldiers behind her were howling and cheering her.

She started screaming at us, saying, "You insolent people! Because of you, you vile people, I lost my husband! I will kill you the same way you killed him! You will pay! I swear you will pay!" She hiccupped and went upstairs.

We were scared and horrified by her threat. Jadra was a woman of her word. If she said that she would kill us, then she could definitely kill us! The soldiers who saw her outburst laughed among themselves. Then they howled and said, "Look at that! Is she dumb, or is she pretending she didn't know?"

"What do you mean?" another soldier asked the first one. "What happened to her?"

"Nothing happened to that woman. She is a cunning woman," the first soldier answered. "Didn't you know? No one killed her husband. He actually left her because of her bad behavior."

We turned toward each other, aware that she had lied to us so that she could threaten us the way she wanted. If living with the soldiers was a nightmare, then living with Jadra was hell. She was a woman herself but didn't care about people who were of the same gender. She had repeatedly shown us how immoral she was. She didn't care about other religions, nor did she care about their beliefs. In Ramadan, Jadra would make us eat pork all the time.

Pork is forbidden to be eaten in our religion, but she would still force it down our throats. They torched us by making us eat pork. She would often say to us, "All of you will eat pork for the remaining time."

"Please, it's against our—"

"Shut up! I do not care what you say or how you feel! If you want to survive, you will do what I ask you to!" Jadra would interrupt us.

Jadra would sometimes make us girls drink alcohol, and when one of us would refuse her, she would beat her severely until that girl would be covered in her own blood or when the soldiers intervened. Her evilness wouldn't end there. She ensured that nobody would patch that girl up or provide her with medicine. And God forbid if someone did, they would face hell the next day!

Drago never interfered when Jadra or a soldier would mistreat or assault the girls and me. But I remember Gojo did intervene on one occasion. I didn't understand what he achieved with that. Was he trying to be a superhero? Our savior, who had a gruesome mind? To me, Drago and Gojo were the same; there was no difference between them. They were the incarnation of evil!

Once, Jadra strode toward the room that was assigned to us and, pointing toward Lejla and me, said, "Come on, you two, stand up."

"Where are we going?" I asked her.

Jadra turned and slapped me. She retorted, "Do not question me! Do what I ask you to, understand?"

"Yes," I said quietly.

She then took us to the bathroom, where she made us bathe her. She forced us to wash her body, top to bottom. She ignored the aghast looks on our faces and pushed us to clean her private parts too.

When she was satisfied with torturing us, she looked at me and said, "You stay here." Turning toward Lejla, she said, "You can go."

When Lejla was gone, Jadra told me to stay there and left the bathroom. I was getting anxious; my mind kept roaming around different scenarios.

What is she planning? How is she going to torture me now? She has already done so many horrible things!

A few minutes later, Gaga entered the room, and behind her was Jadra. I was paralyzed. Seeing the smirk on his face made me feel dirty.

What are they planning?

The next thing tarnished my self-confidence.

"Remove your clothes and sit in the bathtub," Jadra ordered me.

"W-what?" I asked, astonished.

"I said, remove your clothes and sit in the bathtub!" she screamed in my face.

I had no choice but to do what she asked. It was either that or death, and I was not ready to die, not yet. Not until I could see my family again.

She made Gaga sit with me in the tub and told us that she would be bathing us. I wanted to vomit right at that moment. How could someone be this heartless? Had she gone so far away in the path of destruction that she didn't know what was right or wrong?

Laughing like a banshee, she poured water on us. I was panicking, not knowing what to do, trying to shield myself from the hot pouring water or shield my body from Gaga's praying hands.

Jadra would purposely throw water in my face, making me suffocate. The water would go into my mouth, making it impossible for me to breathe. I thought I would die that day; the water kept coming at me, and I lost consciousness.

* * *

Hell continued. I was given to a Montenegrin soldier, an older man. She determined which girl would belong to which soldier as if we were little dolls in a display shop.

I never had a say in this. Not to anyone. I blamed myself for everything that happened to me. Why? Because I didn't have the strength to resist. I didn't resist them. I let them do whatever they wanted to do with me. I spent my life blaming myself for not standing up for myself and beating my very existence every time I was assaulted.

One day, Jadra entered the room where all the girls were. She looked at us as if we were below her, an insect that she could crush anytime she wanted to. She had a superior look on her face; her arms were behind her, holding something. Dread filled my heart; my gut feeling told me something was going to happen.

"I have a surprise for you girls!" she exclaimed in a sinister voice. "Do you all want to see it?"

We all gazed at each other; neither of us wanted to avoid her. But knowing her, we would get beaten up if we didn't respond to her.

Frightened, Hana asked her, "What is it?"

"Look at that," Jadra snickered. "Isn't she brave?"

Suddenly she stopped laughing and turned serious. I was startled to see how fast she had changed her expressions—and that too as if she wasn't just laughing before.

"Wash them!" She threw something at us. I flinched from the force when it landed near me.

Glancing at the thing Jadra had thrown, I, along with the girls, stilled. The goose bumps appeared on my skin, and my heartbeat was rapid.

Is she joking?

"Oh, please! Don't be surprised." Jadra rolled her eyes. "It's just the soldiers' uniforms covered in blood." Looking at each of us, she seethed, "Muslim blood."

A shiver went down my spine. Glancing back at the cloth, I started shaking. The little food I had eaten earlier was pushing its way back up my throat. I wanted to puke but knew Jadra was sharply watching us; I forced it back in.

"Come on now!" she shouted. "I don't have all day for you people. I have other things to do. Stand up and go wash these clothes. And remember that there should not be a drop of blood on the uniforms; otherwise, you people know very well what will happen to you!"

We rushed out of the room and went to the laundry room. My gut feeling was right; it was a devastating thing. Jadra was an evil lady; she took pleasure in others' misery. Our pain was her entertainment, her salvage.

"What are we going to do now?" Hana asked.

"What else? We are going to wash these dirty uniforms," Lejla commented.

"But the b-b-blood on the clothes is . . ." Hana trailed off, unable to finish her sentence.

Everyone stopped what they were doing. Each and every one of us could feel the pain the killed people's family was going through. There was a heavy silence in the air.

"I know, but we can't do anything," Lejla muttered.

* * *

At night, soldiers came, choosing girls for themselves. It had become a routine for them. In the day, they would go out and murder the Muslim men and women. Then they would come back and show us their uniform, taking pride in slaughtering innocent people.

They would often mock us by saying that our community was naive and weak, that we were nothing in front of them. And at night, when the soldiers would get bored from tormenting us emotionally, they would then torture us physically. And as I think now, physical torture is way worse than emotional torture. A person can avoid or ignore what people talk about them, but it is sometimes impossible to overcome the physical abuse trauma in one's life.

* * *

"You," a Montenegrin soldier pointed at me one day.

"What's wrong?" Jadra inquired, glaring at me. "What did she do?"

"Nothing," he said. "Just make sure that nobody else touches her. From now on, only I am allowed to be with her."

"Why?" Jadra questioned.

The Montenegrin gazed at her sharply as if he wanted to kill her. He fisted her hair, pulled it, and yelled in her face, "Mind your own business, woman. Don't forget we men are in charge over here, and you are below us!"

Embarrassed that she was degraded in front of the prisoners, she clenched her hand hard and lowered her head, mumbling, "Yes, sir."

Jadra didn't like it. Not one bit. I could see from the look in her eyes that showed how much she hated me. Whenever she would see me, she would pile up chore after chore for me so that I couldn't breathe. But little did she know that I was already dead; I wasn't breathing.

Jadra was searching for a way, something that could help her take revenge on me, and unfortunately, she found one.

One day, in August, when the Montenegrin was on the field, she took me to the ground floor and locked me in a room.

Puzzled, I backed away from the room. I couldn't comprehend why she had locked me in a room alone. But soon I realized I wasn't alone. I could hear someone breathing. Instantly, I turned around and searched the room. A soldier was sitting on the bed; his eyes were scanning my body, haunting me. They called him Phantom; he had a scar on his face.

I knew what was going on. I was paralyzed and didn't fight that time, nor did I scream or cry!

Phantom left the room when he was done tarnishing my soul, laughing. I pushed myself up, wounded and broken. Moving slowly, I pushed the door open and ran toward the bathroom, getting past Jadra, who was laughing at my shattered dignity.

I jumped in the shower, turning it on. Leaning my head on the wall, I glanced down at my bloodied body.

Tears fell from my eyes one by one, and then they constantly felt like a slow tap. Placing my palm on my mouth to stop myself from screaming, I slid down the wall.

I was screaming, but there was no voice.

I scratched all over my body; the nails dug into my skin until they drew blood. I cleaned my body continuously, trying to remove the dirt but to no avail. My skin turned red, and blemishes started to appear on my body. I was hurting myself, but I didn't care about it. The only thing on my mind was to get rid of the filth that was on my body.

I am dirty! I have no worth! the thought kept resonating in my mind again and again.

* * *

At night, the Montenegrin soldier returned and entered the girls' room. Gazing at me, he knew something was wrong. He called Jadra into the room and asked her, "What did you do to her?

"What are you talking about? I . . . I didn't do anything to her," she stammered nervously.

The soldier wasn't a fool, and her stammering gave her away. "Who was with her?" he asked in a low, dark voice.

Jadra lowered her head and refused to answer him.

He shifted his attention to me and asked, "Who were you with?"

I opened my mouth to speak but stopped when my gaze fell on Jadra. Behind his back, Jadra put her thumb on the right side of her neck and moved it to the left. She was telling me that she would slice me if I said anything. Frightened, I shut my mouth and went silent.

The Montenegrin could see I was hesitating because of Jadra. He got furious at her interference, aware that she had given me to another soldier. Spinning back toward her, he roared, "You bitch! I told you, didn't I?" He slapped her. "I told you she was mine! Nobody could touch her, and you disobeyed me!" He stormed out of the room.

After that, Jadra beat me all night while screaming, "Who the hell are you, bitch? Why did I get slapped for you? Huh? Answer me, you useless girl!" She abused me mentally and physically, but the former was worse.

"Oh, Lord, when will I get away from this life?" I silently prayed as the violence continued. "Please help me get away from these monsters."

Chapter 7

Homecoming

When you are faced with a test of faith, stay within the safety
and security of the household of God. There is always a place
for you here. No trial is so large we can't overcome it together.
—Neil L. Andersen

It was on that day that I got freedom from my tormentors. I felt safe
but never secure. There was a constant pressure on my mind that they
would find me someday and I would be dragged back to hell. For years,
I looked behind my shoulder, paranoid that someone was following me.
Whenever someone approached me, I would get startled as if they were
going to harm me.

But for how long would this haunt me? When would I have the
choice to leave this fear behind and live a life where I could be carefree and
at peace?

* * *

On the same night, when Jadra beat me, dozens of soldiers entered
the house. It looked like they were having a celebration; perhaps they were
happy about killing innocent people again! The girls and I were forced to
serve and entertain them. We were assigned the task of cooking a hefty
meal for them.

We all were busy in the kitchen, handing out plates to the soldiers,
when suddenly the soldier Sale entered the room and told Hana to follow

him. Scared for her life, she slowly followed him. He took her to the living room, guided her to a secluded corner, and started talking to her.

"Hey! Can you pass me the bowl?" Lejla asked me.

Turning my attention away from Hana and the soldier, I passed the bowl to Lejla. When I looked back in their direction, I was startled to see that they were gone.

Where did they go?

Neither of us saw Hana after that, not even later when we went to our room. There was no sign of her. It wasn't just us who noticed her disappearance, but the devil too! Jadra knew that Hana and I were close, so when she could not find her, she took out her anger on me and whipped my body violently.

"Where is she?" Jadra kept screaming and slashing my body with the belt.

"I . . . I d-don't k-know!" I whimpered.

"You know where she is! Stop lying! Tell me where has she gone, and I will spare your life!"

But I was unable to answer her!

* * *

The next day, the soldier Sale showed up and entered the girls' room. He asked me to come downstairs to the living room. Unsure of what was going on, I followed him. But before he could step out of the house, he was confronted by Jadra.

"Where is that girl?" she shrieked. "Where did you take her?"

"You don't need to worry about her. I have taken her someplace, she is with others," Sale told her, indifferent.

"Oh, all right." Then she glanced at me and yelled, "What are you doing here? You brat!"

"I am taking her with me."

"Why her?" she asked, glaring at me. "You can take another girl! Any other girl. You can choose whoever you want."

"I want her," he said firmly.

Jadra kept glaring at me as if it was my fault that he was taking me. Sale could feel that Jadra wouldn't let me go easily, so he applied a different method to convince her. He shoved his hands into his pants pocket and took out a bag of money.

"Here," he said, lifting her hand and dropping the money in her palm. "Now stop making a fuss and let us go!" He paid Jadra a hundred German marks and escorted me out of the house.

When I was making my way out of the house, Drago saw us. He didn't utter a word and silently watched us leave; however, as we were bypassing him, he pranced forward, stopping me, and lifted my left hand.

"Wait," Drago said, taking off my mother's ring and passing it to Jadra. "You won't need this anymore." He walked inside the house without looking back, and Sale pushed me toward the car.

"Come on, we don't have all day!"

Throughout the car ride, I kept looking out, worried and scared. Timidly I asked Sale where he was taking me. Sale didn't answer me immediately, but I was glad that he did tell me what was going on!

Hana's father was a powerful German man who had enough money. The soldiers knew this and demanded a ransom from him. So Hana's father had paid for her and her cousin's release.

I was a little surprised as I knew Hana and I were not related. *So why did he take me and not her real family? Is there an ulterior motive behind his action?* I kept thinking about it. However, all my questions were answered when Sale took me to where Hana was staying. It turned out that I had the same name as her cousin. Ironically, yet thankfully, I was saved by mistake!

After staying one night at the place, Sale took us to Belgrade, where Hana's father would meet us. Not being imprisoned in houses around Foca did not mean that I was happy, and it definitely did not mean that I was free. The suffering of a girl whose childhood, dignity, and life were taken away by drunken freaks and the pain and horror I faced in that dreadful place were going to stay with me like a nightmare. They didn't end!

* * *

We stayed in Belgrade for a few days, and then when Hana's father met us, Sale left to go back to the house. Hana told her father that it would be inhumane to leave me behind, even though I was saved by mistake, and that they should take me. But her father refused as he didn't want the Serbs to come after them because of me.

They couldn't take me with them. Hana had wanted to, but she had her own life. And I completely understood her father's reasoning. We hugged each other and wept wholeheartedly, knowing that it would be the last time we would see each other. When they left, I moved forward on my journey. I roamed the streets, trying to find a place, somewhere, anywhere. But everyone would look at me as if I were a beggar and would turn me down harshly.

And why wouldn't they? I wasn't clean, nor was I allowed to take a bath for a week. My clothes were torn and had dry blood on them. My hair was messy and tangled, and there was even dirt under my nails. Defeated and exhausted from the pointed stares, I took shelter in an alley beside a garbage bin. Sitting on the hard floor, I lifted my knees and wrapped my arms around them. Placing my head on my knees, I cried for my unfortunate life.

What is the purpose of my existence? Why do I feel insecure when I am saved from the monsters? What is going to happen now? I don't have any money on me, nobody would even hire me! How am I going to eat or drink?

"Hey!" a voice shouted, making me jump.

Turning my head to the alley entrance, I found an elderly couple looking down at me fondly. After what I had gone through, I didn't want to trust anyone, but there was something in their eyes that made me want to trust them.

"What are you doing here, honey?" the woman asked warmly.

"I . . . I . . ." I was speechless. I couldn't say anything. I just kept on staring at them.

"I think it will be better if we talk about it after you are washed and fed," the old man murmured, smiling. "Would you like to come with us, love? We will watch over you."

I didn't know what to do. I didn't know them. What if they turned out to be just like those demons? However, the light in their eyes and the tender smile on their lips told me otherwise.

"Okay," I nodded.

The couple took me to their house. The wife told me to wash while she would make something for me. After I had washed, I felt a lot better and relaxed. The clean water had purified my body that was covered by dirt. Running my hands through my hair to untangle it, I made my way to the dining table. Upon reaching it, I saw the woman waiting for me with a bowl of chicken soup.

"Come eat, darling," she said, motioning me to sit on the chair. "You need nutrition in your body to fight the world."

"How did you . . . ?" I asked, taking a mouthful of the soup.

"Your eyes, child." She smiled, taking a seat in front of me. "They show that you have gone through pain and suffering." She paused. "I am a mother too. I can feel when a child is troubled and is seeking harmony."

"I . . . I . . ." I swallowed. "They . . . they . . ."

I burst out crying and told her everything from the beginning to the end. I didn't leave anything veiled; I showed her my scorching scars. And that woman, she wrapped me in her arms, caressing my head, comforting me.

"What are you going to do now, love?"

"I am thinking of going to Ruma, Serbia. I want to find my mother and brothers."

"Will it be safe? Won't you get caught by the soldiers?"

"I don't know, Aunt. I have no choice but to take the risk."

"All right, I will support you in whatever decision you make, but remember, if you are in trouble, you can always come back to me." She kissed my forehead.

"All right, I will."

"Also, while you live in Serbia, remember, you must not say who you are no matter what happens. You must give yourself a Serbian name," she cautioned me.

I stayed with the elderly couple for a few days. They helped me in every way they could, from nourishing me to helping me adjust to reality. And when it was time to leave, they gave me a small bag of money that would help me in my journey.

* * *

I went to Ruma, Serbia, believing that I would find neighbors from Miljevina. But unfortunately, I never found them, and my desperation was fueled. It was naive of me to think that they would still be living there. I didn't, for a second, think that the war had affected them too.

Following the advice of the elderly woman, I gave myself a Serbian name. Since then, the fight of a sixteen-year-old girl who was hiding behind a false name started in the villages around Ruma. Fighting for her livelihood, she worked in cafés and bars around the place.

I started working in different cafés in a row, moving from one to another. The first place I worked at was a restaurant. I was assigned to wash dishes. And so, I worked hard, day and night, washing the dirty dishes. It was my only way of earning money. Later on, I also trained myself on how to be a waitress.

Even though the environment and pay were good, I didn't linger in restaurants and cafés for long. I constantly changed the places I used to stay at. I thought that I could save myself by doing this and it would be difficult to find me. It was also easier for me to run away in case the soldiers searched for me.

People tried to be friendly toward me; they would try to get close to me, but I would remain wary of them. I did not want anyone to know about me, fearing that someone would realize that I was posing a false identity and that it would cause problems. And it was later when I realized that whatever I had thought was true!

One day, when the people found out who I was and where I was from, they started threatening me—calling me names and insulting me. The people soon realized that I had come to their country to save myself. It didn't take long for them to identify who I was. Also, my birth certificate was with the UNPROFOR (United Nations Peacekeepers), on which my real name was written. It meant a new danger to me. I had to run.

* * *

My next destination was Montenegro. I managed to escape to Montenegro when they realized who I was in Serbia. It was peaceful for a few days, without having to worry about anything. But that peace only lasted for some weeks, and dread surrounded my life again.

Since Montenegro was located between the border of Bosnia and Foca, the Serbs kept coming to visit the city. I thought that as long as I didn't come across them, I would be safe. I would hide my face whenever they would pass by me or change my route if I saw them walking on the same path. But alas! It didn't work out.

One day, they recognized me, and then the threats started all over again. It was torturous for me to hear their words, but I had to swallow the poison if I wanted to survive. I met the soldiers who abused me, and seeing them again terrorized me. One by one, the abusers and murderers arrived in Montenegro looking for me, trying to take me back to the city where I had gone through hell.

In Montenegro, before the signing of the Dayton Agreement, I lived under house arrest, as my identity had been discovered by the Serbian soldiers and people. I was just a girl who survived with a false name and spoke Serbian to fit in better!

* * *

During the years of struggle for existence, I established contact with my lost family. I desperately wanted to see them, to be near them, and to be able to live with them again. There wasn't a single time when I didn't miss them; they were with me at every step of my life. Not physically, but mentally and emotionally.

I started looking for my mom and brothers through the Red Cross, but every letter I sent would get returned to me. I didn't know if they were still living in our house in Foca or if they had changed their location to some other place.

I was clueless and lost. I was upset and heartbroken! After countless failed attempts, I gave up. I lost hope that I would ever see them again! And one day, after four years, a miracle happened; the moment I had been yearning for came.

In the afternoon, when I came back from work, I got a call from my teacher.

"I have seen your letter, child," she said. "I know where your mom and brothers are. I can help you get in touch with them."

The teacher's call was like a blessing for me. She provided me with the address of the house where my family was living. Without waiting for a minute, I immediately sent a letter through the Red Cross to the address she had given me.

After a couple of weeks, I received a letter with instructions on how I should talk to my mom through the military station. Excited to hear their voice again, I dialed the number and waited. I sucked in a deep breath when the call was picked up from the other side.

"Hello," a deep male voice answered the call. "Is this . . . ?"

I couldn't understand whom I was talking to! Who is this? Did I call the wrong place? And how do they know my name?

"Hello, may I know who I am talking to?" I asked.

"It is me! Don't you recognize me, sister?"

A tear dropped from my eyes when I realized that I was finally talking to my brother. I was amazed that even after so long, he could easily recognize my voice.

"Have you forgotten about me?" he asked, his voice sorrowful.

My brother had grown up into a young man, and I no longer knew who he was! The monsters had snatched everything from me, even the precious time when I could see him grow up. I had come so far away, losing many memories, that it would take time to go back to how things were!

"No! It's not like that! How could I even forget about you?" I whimpered. "I-it's j-just . . . it's just that it has been so long since I heard your voice."

"I don't blame you, sis."

"Where is Mom? Is she beside you? Can I talk to her? I have missed her so much! I want to hear her voice again—"

"I am sorry, sister." He paused. "Even if I want to, I couldn't help you to talk to her."

"Why? What is it? Did something happen to her?"

"No, no. She is fine, nothing happened to her." I sighed in relief and was about to ask him again when he replied, "M-Mom couldn't gather enough strength to talk to you. She blames herself for what happened to you."

"B-but it wasn't! I-it was my f-fault. I deserved i-it."

"No, sister! It wasn't anyone's fault, and neither did you deserve it!" he shouted, breathing heavily. Then he lowered his voice and said, "Especially not yours."

But I couldn't believe him. I knew he was just saying that to comfort me. I blamed myself for everything!

"Don't worry, everything is going to be all right. You are going to be here with us again. And I promise we will hear from each other again," he told me.

That night, I couldn't sleep. I cried continuously. Whenever I would try to wipe the tear, a new set of tears would flow from my eyes. Dreadful thoughts revolved around my mind. It was the first time that I doubted if my family was going to accept me. After all, I was now a girl who was damaged, and that too beyond repair.

* * *

After my family found out that I was alive and safe, I was immediately contacted by a relative living in France at that time. From that day on, everything was easier. The relative and I remained in touch, and she would often send me money. Her father, who was also my uncle, had a close Serbian friend, Matija. Matija used to travel from Bosnia to Montenegro for business purposes. My uncle asked him if he could help and take me back to Bosnia after the war had ended.

Matija was a humble and kind guy; he accepted my uncle's request and helped me get back to Bosnia. In the short journey, he treated me as his daughter; never once did he make me feel unsafe. I would forever be grateful to the man who made my dream of reconciling with my family come true.

When I arrived in Bosnia, and as soon as I reached the border, I called my uncle. Since he was not there and his wife could not leave the store, she called my other uncle. It was his daughter who answered the phone, and I was told that my cousin would be receiving me. It was later on that I learned that my cousin was so overjoyed to see me that as soon as my aunt told her that I had arrived, she threw the phone away and ran outside the house to pick me up.

When my cousin arrived to pick me up, I couldn't recognize who she was. I was confused. I had never seen her, so who was she? But the moment she smiled, I realized who she was. My cousin had been little when the war started, and now that I was seeing her after so many years, she had grown up so well. The wide smile on her face told me that she was happy to see me, but I looked at her as if she was a stranger.

My reaction was basically true as I didn't really know who she was. The lost years had built a wall between my family and me, making me a stranger. My cousin didn't let me hold anything, insisting that I needed to rest and relax. She picked up my things in her small hands, and we headed to her house. Before we could reach her house, we met my uncle halfway on the roadside. He was coming to meet us, and that was the first time I saw him cry.

My uncle had always been a brave guy; he would be the first one who would volunteer to help someone in need. My parents would tell me how courageous he was that even in a difficult situation, he would never shed a tear and would fight it head-on.

When we arrived in front of my uncle's apartment building, a large crowd had already gathered outside, waiting. My other uncles were also standing outside, discussing how to let my mother know that I had arrived.

It was decided that one of them would go beforehand and tell her about me. And that I would arrive after she had calmed down. So my uncle, along with his wife, drove to my mom's house with sedatives as a precaution. After a while, my other uncle took me with him in his car.

We arrived at the street where my mom and brothers were currently living. The street was full of people, but they were all strangers to me. They were looking at me as if they knew me, with a smile on their face; they were cheering for me.

My mother later on told me, "During the war, I had talked about you nonstop to every other person I met. I would tell them how you were and what you used to do. And the best part was that they all loved how amazing you were." She stroked my hair. "All these people met you through me. People would come to the house, asking if you had sent any letters. They all looked forward to every letter I received from you just as I used to."

It was an emotional reunion. I was surrounded by my mother and brothers. We cried while hugging each other tightly. They kept on asking me if I was okay or if I wanted something. My mother prepared my favorite dishes for me and complained that I had become thin while my brother was at my beck and call.

"Thank you for bringing her back," my mother told my uncles.

"There is no need to thank us, sister. She is our family too, we all love her as our own," one of my uncles spoke on behalf of everyone. Soon they went back to their houses.

My brothers, especially the elder one, wouldn't let me step outside, nor would he let me slip away from his eyes in fear that I would disappear again.

He would sometimes tell me, "Sister, you do not have to worry about anything. You are safe now, nothing bad will ever happen to you. I am your brother, sister. I was young and naive at that time, but now I have grown up and can protect you. You do not have to fear anything; I am going to keep you safe."

For months, I felt lost; it felt unreal to me, as if I weren't there. It was as if I were watching a movie and as if everything were happening to someone other than me.

It took me a long time to realize that I was no longer alone and had someone to count on.

* * *

I have observed that in everyone's life, there are both good and bad things. The same applies to people. If there are virtuous and kind people in this world, then there are wicked and sinful people.

And I realized it a little too late!

Since I had changed my way of speaking in addition to the name to fit in Serbia, it took me a while to return to the Bosnian dialect.

While I was working on my Bosnian dialect, people would always insult me. I understood them in a way because the war was just over, and people were angry at everything that was happening.

It didn't bother me at first, but when I first went to town on the bus, I met a guy who went with me to the elementary school. I was happy to see him, to know that he was alive and well. I was delighted that I met someone I had known from before the war.

I was living in a fairy tale, thinking that everything had gone back to how things had been. I thought that, like my family, people would also accept me and still treat me like how they used to. But I had forgotten the fact that if I wasn't the same girl that I used to be, then how come they would behave the same way?

My nonexistent fantasy was broken when the guy turned toward me and shouted, "Serbian whore!" His eyes had a fire in them. "All of this happened because of you! It's all your fault!"

I was distraught that instead of being friendly toward me, he started insulting me. It was a horrible experience for me, but instead of learning from that, I ignored it, thinking that maybe the guy wasn't in a good mood and it was my fault for approaching him.

When I started regaining consciousness about my surroundings, I started going out with friends. I met a guy I really liked, and I started dating him. I didn't tell anyone what had happened to me because I was ashamed of everything. At that time, I had started blaming myself for everything because that was how people treated me.

One day, after a week of going out with him, we were sitting on the beach and enjoying our date. I built up the courage and told him about what had happened, thinking that he would understand me and would love me no matter what. But the unexpected happened!

His mood turned upside down, and he scowled as if he had eaten something sour. Immediately he told me, "We are over."

"What? What are you talking about?" I exclaimed.

"I said, we are over! I don't think I can be with you anymore!"

"But why? What happened? Was it something I said?"

"Why? You are asking me why!" he shouted. "As if you don't know why I am doing this! How could you even imagine I will stay with you?"

"I really don't understand. I am seriously lost." I cried.

"So you want to pretend that you don't know! All right, I will tell you!" he yelled. "I cannot bear that my girlfriend had gone through something so disgusting! How could you do something so obnoxious?"

"I . . . I didn't! I . . . I was f-forced—"

"Yeah, right! People like you don't get forced!"

"W-what do you m-mean?"

"Nothing, just let it go! I am breaking up with you. I could not be with such an awful girl like you!"

At that moment, something broke inside me, and I promised myself that I would never again hide what had happened to me! When I would find a person I liked in the future, I would tell him everything right away because I would rather lose him in the beginning rather than go through the same disappointment again.

"Let him go, sister. He was not the one for you," my brother consoled me, letting me borrow his shoulder to cry. Our relationship had become stronger than before, up to the point where I could tell him and find comfort in him. "You will meet him one day. The one who would cherish you and love you wholeheartedly."

It was then that I understood that we could never hold on to people. It's no use to force them to be with us; the people who will love and care for you would never abandon you under any circumstances. My family is the perfect example of those people!

* * *

When the war was over, the soldiers who tormented me were arrested and taken into custody. When I heard the news, I decided to testify; even though I had no self-confidence, I wanted to prove to people that I was not a bad person. I wanted to let them know that I was the victim; I was forced and imprisoned. I also wanted to show the whole world that the Serbs were to blame for everything and not me.

Fate would determine that in the courtroom of The Hague Tribunal, I would meet those who destroyed my life, looking them in the eye and relating all the atrocities they committed.

Chapter 8

The First Testimony

Fear keeps us focused on the past or worried about the future.
If we can acknowledge our fear, we can realize that right now;
we are okay. Right now, today, we are still alive, and our bodies
are working marvelously. Our eyes can still see the beautiful
sky. Our ears can still hear the voices of our loved ones."
—Thich Nhat Hanh

In 1995, North Atlantic Treaty Organization enforced a cease-fire in Dayton, Ohio, to stop the war in Bosnia and Herzegovina. A peace treaty was signed between the presidents of Bosnia, Croatia, and Serbia.

One by one, the people who were behind the war were arrested and put on trial. On March 4, 1998, Drago surrendered himself and was taken into custody for his crimes in the war.

* * *

A year had gone by since I got reunited with my family, but I was still fighting to adjust to reality. The people never quit insulting or humiliating me, but I could endure it knowing that I had my family with me. I was not going to give up and stop living just because people didn't want me to.

This was my life. Only I knew what I had been through; no one could tell me to do otherwise. The first time I heard the news related to Drago's surrender, I was both relieved and shocked. The war had ceased, but the ghost of what had happened remained with all of us. It was a constant reminder of what my life had gone through.

I remember it was a Thursday night when my family and I were watching a late-night show. We huddled around in the living room after having our dinner. After the show ended, my youngest brother started telling me about his school life, and my other brother, older than the youngest one, kept shuffling the channels. Our mother was watching us with a faint smile on her face; she had a sorrowful look in her eyes.

Without asking her, I could understand what she was feeling at that time. As a woman who had lost her husband, seeing that her children were alive and healthy made her emotional.

"My friends and I just wanted to play," my youngest brother said, sulking. "Why did we get punished?"

"Obviously, you will get punished," my other brother replied, "if you start to play in the middle of the class and not pay attention to the teacher."

"But . . ." My younger brother paused and looked at me. "Was I wrong, sister?"

"Hmm . . ." I trailed off, thinking. "Big Brother is right, we shouldn't be playing when we are in the class."

"All right, I—"

"Yesterday, on March 4, the leader of a reconnaissance unit of the Bosnian Serb Army, Drago surrendered . . ."

The report on the news channel halted everyone in their tracks. My breathing hitched, and my eyes widened in shock. I couldn't believe what I was seeing. The police force was dragging the man who had been behind all this, with handcuffs on his hands.

"S-sister?" I heard my oldest brother calling out to me, but the fog of fear that covered my mind stopped me from answering him. "Sister!" Panicking, he shook my shoulders.

"Huh?" When I became conscious of my surroundings, I saw my brothers kneeling beside me wearing alarmed expressions. My mother was standing behind them, hovering above us, worry evident in her eyes.

"Are you all right, child?" my mother asked me, stroking my head tenderly.

I was unable to speak, too numb to think about anything. So I only nodded, trying to assure them; however, it was clear that they weren't convinced. To distract me, my mother and brothers changed the subject and started talking about the upcoming dinner we were attending at one of my uncles' houses.

I barely interacted with them at that time, speaking only when someone would ask me a question. I was with them, but my mind was somewhere else. Even when I placed my head on the pillow that night, my eyes were getting deprived of sleep, but my mind kept revolving around disturbing thoughts.

What is going on?

Why did he surrender?

What is the reason behind it?

Was he forced, or is it a new horrible game he wants to play with his victims?

* * *

Days went on slowly, and the news of Drago's surrender spread quickly throughout the town. The questions that had deliberately stopped started coming again. They behaved like hyenas who wanted to tear apart my happiness.

People would stop and ask me how I felt now and what I would do now. Their attitude was making me more panicked and afraid. It was like I was again trapped in that place and suffocating in the hollow darkness.

"What are you going to do, cousin?" my cousin asked me one day when we were sitting outside in her garden.

"What do you mean?" I asked, confused.

"I heard the court and advocates are searching for witnesses against Drago."

"Oh!" I stared at her, trying to understand where she was going with this. "I . . . I don't understand what you are trying to say."

"It's just . . . " She paused, trying to figure out how to word it. "Many people have come forward to testify in court. A-are you also going to testify?"

"I don't know," I said, sighing. "I don't want anything to do with him. The nightmares haven't stopped yet, and I don't want them to surface again."

"But don't you think he needs to suffer for what he had put you people through! That man should be imprisoned for life."

"I know, I want him to suffer too, but I don't think I can face him in court. I don't have the courage to answer the questions the prosecutor will be asking me," I stated. "So no, I will not testify."

"All right, if you think that is good for you, then I won't force you." She nodded, agreeing with me.

But I could see in her eyes that she wanted me to but couldn't convey her thoughts to me in case she might hurt me. I knew that people around me, my family and friends, walked on eggshells. At that time, I desperately wished for things to go back to normal.

My cousin wasn't the only one who asked me if I would be going to testify. Relatives, friends, neighbors, and even strangers asked if I wanted to testify, but I would always refuse.

I knew testifying would mean facing him again, seeing his wicked smile and haunting eyes. He wasn't my assaulter, no, but he was the one who initiated it in the first place, and I hated him for that.

Hate is a prominent word; it has a deeper meaning behind it. Before all this, I was a girl who never got furious or held a grudge against anyone. I would always forget and forgive people, moving on with my life. But how could I forgive the monsters who destroyed my willpower and made me a shell-shocked person?

The devils never regretted or felt bad for what they were doing to innocent people. They were the beasts who would just laugh at us, mocking, insulting, and humiliating us. Gradually, I heard that the girls whom Drago had tormented started to appear as witnesses. In the comfort of my home, I was keenly observing the case, wanting to know if we would get justice or be set free.

In the meantime, I was also visiting the psychologists that were assigned to me. They tried to help me by making me open up about my wounds, but unfortunately, every time I tried to talk about them, it would provoke me as the scars were still fresh.

One day, one of my physiologists said, "I know it hurts you, but to move on in your life, you need to acknowledge that you have been hurt. That it wasn't an awful dream but your reality," she paused. "I assume you're obliged to come forward as a responsible civilian and do the needful."

"I beg your pardon?"

"It's about time you give your testimony on the matter and protect the younger generation from power-hungry predators."

I told her that I would keep her words in mind and would think about it thoroughly. Her words kept revolving in my mind, but I didn't think much of it until I met some of the captured girls.

"I want to see him behind bars," Esma said when I met them at a local park. "He has done so much damage to our life, he needs to be punished."

"I agree with you!" Asla said.

"I also agree that they need to be punished, but I am a little afraid to give my testimony," I declared.

"Afraid of what?" Asla asked.

"What if they are set free and not found guilty? We all know how powerful they are. Who would believe in us?" I expressed my worries.

"I can understand where you are coming from, but don't worry," Esma said. "My father had found out that they will be giving witness protection to the victims. He told me that we will be safe, and it's not just us, thousands of people will be giving their testimony."

It was then that I realized that testifying was the only way to make me feel better, and the most important thing was that these war criminals needed to pay for everything they did.

While learning about the law and custody, I learned that molestation was never a war crime, and our role was important in it. If we hadn't given our testimony, many women would have suffered to get justice. After our testimony, the UN court characterized sexual assault as a war crime for the first time in history!

* * *

It was a difficult decision for me, but I went to the international court in The Hague because of the unlimited support and aid from my family and friends. The officers told me to wait in a room where the other witnesses were already gathered. In that room, four security guards and police officers were stationed for our protection.

One at a time, the witnesses were called to the courtroom. While in the waiting room, we could hear people talking in the courtroom, but the voices were inaudible, making it impossible to understand what was going on. My hands were continuously shaking, and the uncontrollable sweating made my palms clammy. My heart was beating at a faster rate, making it hard for me to breathe. I tried my best to take a shallow, slow breath but to no avail.

At that time, I insisted on going on my own because I thought I was strong enough and that nothing could break me anymore. I remembered my brother had insisted on going with me, but I had refused him as I didn't want him to know about the horrors his dear sister had gone through. I knew it would've devastated him if he knew what had happened at the detention camps.

"Let me go with you," he had pleaded. "I will be there beside you and support you."

"No, it's okay," I told him, caressing his hair. "I want to go alone."

"Sis . . ." He paused. "You know you don't have to endure it alone anymore. Your family is with you now, we have your back and will help you in every step of your life."

"I know, but . . ." I hesitated. "Don't worry, your sister is brave enough to face every kind of monster now. They won't let me overpower me."

"Promise?"

"I promise."

But I was mistaken.

It was around half past two in the afternoon when my witness number was called. The walk to the courtroom was dreadful. My body didn't have any strength to move forward; it was as if I was dragging myself.

I entered the courtroom for the first time, and involuntarily, my eyes met the criminals. Seeing their emotionless eyes made me suck in a breath, and I began to shake uncontrollably. I stood still in my place, stuck in that position, contemplating if I should move forward or run out of the courtroom.

I can't recall how I managed to walk in front of the courtroom or sit down on the witness stand. When I regained consciousness again, I found myself in front of the judge. Taking a deep breath to calm myself, I recited the oath:

"I solemnly declare upon my honor and conscience that I will speak the truth, the whole truth and nothing but the truth."

Luckily, the prosecutor was in charge for the first time, and she was leading the testimony. Without looking in the direction of Drago and the other soldiers once, I gathered my strength and answered her questions.

Initially, she asked me basic questions about myself, my family, and how everything started. All the witnesses were given a pseudonym; we were not allowed to call them out by their names to hide their identities.

"While you were in Miljevina, what were the living conditions for the Muslims? Were they allowed to roam freely, and was there food available for them?" the prosecutor asked me.

"We couldn't move around freely, there were restrictions everywhere. Also, we didn't have a lot of food as we were under house arrest."

"All right. Please tell me if this was a public order. Did the government ask that you stay in the house? Also, why did you feel you were under house arrest? Were there some measures taken by the Serb soldiers? Do you know who that someone was who ordered you to stay at home, and how?"

"I don't really know about this, they just locked us in without telling us everything. I am unable to answer this question as I can't recall it."

"And what about the Serb neighbors? Did they also have to go through the same treatment, and were they deprived of food?" she asked.

"No, the restrictions did not apply to them. The neighbors had enough food."

The questions continued; she kept asking me for information about what I had seen or heard in the detention house. I was starting to relax a little when the prosecutor asked a question I was dreading.

"Can you describe Drago?" the prosecutor inquired.

"H-he is tall, thin, with long, curly brown hair, has a deep voice and big rounded eyes," I replied hesitatingly, knowing that he was right there, looking at me with his penetrating eyes.

I could feel the heat of his deep-rooted heated glare at the side of my face. You can do it! I kept telling myself. He won't do anything to you.

"Could you please look around and tell us if the man Drago, or Drago, is here?"

I turned my head slightly toward the left and slowly glanced around the room. My eyes stopped at the person sitting casually and in an uninterested manner right next to the security guard. Drago. My gut feeling was right; he was glaring at me, warning me.

"Y-yes, h-he's here," I told the prosecutor, turning toward her.

"All right. Can you please tell the court where he is sitting?" she asked.

"Uh . . . f-from my left, h-he is sitting next to the g-guard." I swallowed nervously.

She asked to reflect and take into their notice that I recognized the accused person. After that, the avoidable questions came one after the other, making it difficult for me to cope with them. The prosecutor unveiled my hideous old wounds, asking me about what I had endured at the detention camps and whether I was abused or harmed in any way.

Hearing her questions, I tried to block the memories from resurfacing, making it harder for me to describe everything in-depth. It took a long time to answer; the prosecutor had to help me in between it as I could not say some words aloud. I had a feeling that if I said everything out loud and publicly, then everything would become irrelevant and that I would be the one to blame for everything and the one who was not good enough.

My hands were clasped tightly, nervously; the nails were digging into the back of my hands. It was difficult for me to stop the tears that were fighting to break free. I felt ashamed and embarrassed when I told them about the assaults. I couldn't lift my head and look at anyone, afraid that they would have a disgusting and loathing look on their faces.

* * *

After that first day, the prosecutor told me that the next time I testified and Drago's lawyers asked me questions, I must have someone close to me. She told me that the cross-questioning could be harsh and that I should have someone to help me go through it.

"The prosecutor told me to bring someone with me when Drago's lawyer would be asking the questions next time," I explained to my family.

My brother was about to volunteer when I shook my head, halting him. He was a little upset, but he supported me in my decision after I explained that I was only doing this for his own good as I did not want him to get hurt. A relative who was closer to me lived in Paris at the time. When she heard about my testimonies and that I was looking for someone to go with for the next one, she immediately flew down to Bosnia to support and be with me.

With her arrival, everything was easier, and thanks to her, I gathered my strength and continued my testimony.

* * *

Some of the crimes that Drago committed were the following:

Sexual assaults and torture of girls. It was recognized as a crime against humanity and a violation of the laws.

The enslavement of girls in different locations. It was recognized as a crime against humanity.

On February 22, 2001, he was sentenced to twenty-eight years of imprisonment, and the next year in December, he was transferred to Germany.

The eagle has no fear of adversity. We need to be like the eagle
and have the fearless spirit of a conqueror!
—Joyce Meyer

Chapter 9

The Start of Something New

The ache for home lives in all of us, the safe place where we can
go as we are and not be questioned.
—Maya Angelou

After I went to The Hague to testify, witness support told me that
it would be best to leave Bosnia because they thought I was no longer
safe there. I had the right to choose the country I wanted to go to and get
citizenship in, but it would be only me and not my family who would get
the citizenship.

"America," I told them after a lot of consideration and thoughtfulness.

I chose to go to America as it was the only country providing residency
for my family and me. Not only that, but the United States of America
was also offering a safe passage to my family and me. I had an uncle who
lived over there, so I knew it would be the best choice for me to move over
there. There was a program helping us to move to America; they did all the
paperwork for me and called my family.

The court sent a letter to the American organization with all the
information. While I was in The Hague giving my testimony, my mother
and brothers went through the interviews. When I returned home, I went
through an interview as well.

I had one interview with an American guy who was in charge of the
whole process of moving us to America. The officers didn't ask me a lot of
questions. He already had all the information from the court, and I just
had to confirm my testimony.

The procedure was completed immediately, and we got all the papers within a month. The officers booked us a flight, and we reached America with all the safety and security measures.

"Mom, where are we going?" my youngest brother asked when we were packing one day.

"We are shifting to the USA, my child," my mother replied, smiling faintly.

"Why?" he inquired innocently. "And do we have to?"

"Because . . . ," my mother started explaining the reason for our sudden move to my youngest brother.

"Don't worry," my other younger brother murmured and looked at me, "he will understand, someday. It isn't your fault, it was supposed to go this way."

A warm feeling entered my heart, astonished that my brother had understood what I was feeling and was reassuring me. *He has really grown up so well! I thought. It's a bit upsetting that I couldn't see his growth from a boy to a young man.*

"All right," I nodded.

The days passed in a blur. We got busy packing and visiting our close family and friends. We never knew when we would come back here again, so it was a bittersweet farewell for us. I didn't even know if I wanted to!

My family and I were happy because at that moment, the war in Bosnia had just ended, and everything was taking a long time to get back to normal.

The people who were involved in torturing us and making our lives a complete hell were running loose. My mother thought that moving from the country was the best option for us as we did not want to encounter them.

* * *

I still remember the day when I arrived in America, a country where I would start my life again. It was a fresh start for me; however, the guilt of leaving my father behind alone stayed in my mind. I was a little sad that we had to move from the place we had been born and bred in, but there were no other options.

The threats after the testimony were increasing. People and friends whom I knew were getting furious that I had testified against someone they had thought of as a war hero. They didn't care about the impact their words had on me—the victim.

But now that I had started to walk on the path of redemption, nothing and no one could stop me. I wanted justice for the sins the Serbs had committed toward us. I was not going to back down from any treat now. The program that had helped us move had already arranged an apartment when we arrived in America. It wasn't a big, luxurious one but a small, cozy one that gave me a homely feeling.

For months, our house remained empty; there was no furniture in our home. The whole family would sleep in one big room on a woolen comforter to keep ourselves warm. For a long time, we remained homesick as the new country was unfamiliar territory to us. We took time to adjust to our surroundings.

The uncle who lived in the country assisted us as much as possible; he would send us money every month to not let us die from starvation. We were thankful to him but knew that we had to do something for ourselves.

The neighbors and people we met were amiable; the hospitality my family and I received from them would forever remain in my mind. I didn't know if I could ever meet people other than family who would like to get associated with me without knowing me.

They told us the basics of the town as we were unaware of the rules and regulations. Some of the people I met were of my age; they assisted in touring the town so that my brother and I could become familiar with the area.

There was a church nearby our place, where people donated their belongings that could help other people. One day, some of the people, along with the minister, visited us. My mother and I were perplexed by their sudden appearance as we had never interacted with them. I couldn't help getting suspicious of them, doubting their intention. I had a hard time trusting people.

"Hello," the minister greeted politely. "How are you people doing?"

"Hello, please come inside," my mother said, inviting them into the house.

The minister, along with two men and three women, entered my house. They all had friendly smiles on their faces, but at that time to me, they looked like pretended ones.

One of the women had a large bowl in her hands. She extended it to my mother and said, "Please take this. I made some chicken casserole for you."

"Oh! You shouldn't have, but thank you for the kind hospitality," my mother stated, taking the dish from the woman.

The people settled down and introduced themselves; the minister, James, and his sister, May, had lived in this town since they were born. The woman who had given us the dish, Penny, and her husband, Liam, lived two blocks away from us and were very friendly. The other couple, Miles and Casey, were newlyweds and lived near the church.

"How are you liking the town?" Penny asked, smiling. "I hope you are comfortable over here."

"We are getting adjusted," my mother said. "It's just that it is our first time coming to the USA, but my children and I love the environment over here."

"That's good to know," Casey beamed. "If you ever want to tour the town or want to know anything about the town, just let me know. I will help you in any way I can!"

"Thank you," I replied, smiling faintly.

"Uh, actually, we are here for a reason," the minister hesitated, making me and my brother stiff.

I knew it! I thought, panicked. I knew it! They do have harmful intentions! They are going to do something! What do they want? What is the reason behind their appearance? Why—

"We understand that it must be hard for you to move here so suddenly. We wanted to help you by giving you some furniture and household items," Miles told us, interrupting my thoughts.

"What?" my brother asked, shocked. "Wait, I don't get it."

"The church has a custom that whenever someone moves into the town, we donate something necessary to them that will help them get settled to the place," May explained. "So please do not worry about anything, and allow us to do the hard work."

"B-but how can we accept this?" my mother said, worrying, and looked at my brother and me. "T-this is a lot."

"You do not have to worry," Liam said. Seeing that my mother was still in doubt, he said, "Please at least take it until you or your children have started earning for yourselves."

"All right," my mother agreed.

"But . . . " I paused, making everyone turn their attention toward me. "But how did you people know that we moved here suddenly?" I asked, nervous.

D-do they know where we are from? Do they k-know what happened to me? H-how?

"Oh, that!" Casey smiled. "A week ago, when we were attending the sermon at the church, we heard it from the town people. They told us about you people, and we thought of visiting you."

Oh! I thought, instantly remembering the time when we had first moved in and the excuse we had given to our neighbors when they had asked us the reason for coming here. The excuse was simple: it was to get higher studies.

I nodded. And it was then that I finally realized that they were different from the monsters who had hurt me.

My previous doubts were cleared. The minister and the people proved me wrong; they showed me that there were still good people in the world. It's just that we have to search for them!

* * *

Another compassionate event we went through was when a couple with a two-year-old baby visited our apartment. We didn't really know them; we had heard about the couple from our friends and neighbors.

That was the only time I had met Mr. and Mrs. Grayson. They were a good-natured couple who would help anyone without any hesitation. I would always remember their kind gesture toward us in those trying days.

"I know it might sound really weird, but we wanted to donate our car to you people," Mr. Grayson said while sipping tea.

"Huh?" my mother mumbled. "B-but why?"

"And what would you people be using then, if you give your car to us?" my brother asked, puzzled.

Grayson chuckled and said, "We have three cars. One's mine and the other one is my wife's. The third car I got was an inheritance from my grandfather. So it is extra for us, as both of us use ours."

"We thought it would be better if we could give this car to somebody else," Kate, his wife, said, smiling. "And what better option could we have than you people?"

"Uh, this is huge," I said, unsure. "I don't know if we could accept it."

"Please, it will make us feel good, knowing that our neighbors are not troubled anymore," Grayson said.

"Are you sure you people are okay with it?" my mother asked again.

"Yes, do not worry," Kate replied.

"Thank you for the hospitality," I said. "We will never forget the favor you did for us."

"No, no. Don't be," Kate murmured. "It is a huge pleasure for us to help you."

Two days later, the couple brought a maroon car to our house. It was a simple, furnished car, one that my family fell in love with. Mr. and Mrs. Grayson handed us the car keys along with the necessary equipment for the car.

Although it wasn't a modern and high-tech car, my family and I were attached to it as it was our first car. Over the years that we lived there, we created many beautiful memories with that vehicle.

* * *

Fellow Americans recognized my desire and will to fit in, and they saw how hard I was trying. So they too wanted to help as much as they could. They would often tell me encouraging things that would motivate me to move forward in life. Their words would remain positive, telling me that there would always be better and worse days in people's lives.

I remember a girl I befriended, Macy. Macy was two years older than me and also my neighbor. She would always call me Angel as, according to her, I looked like an angel.

"You are an amazing girl," Macy told me while we were sitting on the swings at a nearby park.

"I wish I could be like you, Macy." I sighed. "I don't have the confidence you have. I am just a simple girl who is trying to live her life peacefully."

"Angel," she said and paused, staring at me intensely, "I don't know what you have gone through in your life, and I promise I won't be asking you about it, but please do not let yourself down like this."

"I don't know, Macy," I told her, dejected from my past experiences. "I doubt if I can do anything."

"Don't be!" she reprimanded me, frowning. "You unnecessarily doubt yourself! You have so much potential, girl. I know you can do wonders if you just believe in yourself!"

I stared at her, trying to find a reason that could help me understand how she was able to see something good in me when I myself was revolted by my existence!

I was a little frustrated too as to how they couldn't see the stain of blood that surrounded me. Why could they see the brightness in my life? What was left inside me that made them believe I could live a happy and carefree life?

"Hey, Angel! Are you even listening to me?" Macy said. "Where are you lost in? Let me know too so we can both get lost in your thoughts!" She laughed.

The wrinkle near her eyes and the vibrant smile made me realize that it wasn't their fault. No one knew what I had gone through, not even my family, so how could I get irritated with them? They didn't know that the light had left me a long time ago and it was darkness that consumed me. I was an empty shell that was trying to find her purpose in life. Bit by bit, with the help of Macy and my other friends, I started to gain some confidence. I was learning to live my life again, peacefully and harmoniously.

* * *

When we first arrived there, none of us spoke English, nor did we know how to write or understand the language. We faced difficulty when we tried to communicate with neighbors and friends. I didn't want to fall behind and stick out like a sore thumb, so I practiced speaking and writing the language.

Once we got a little bit accustomed to the language, my brother and I started applying for jobs. It wasn't easy for us to get employed, especially me, as I was still afraid to go out into the world and face the cruel reality.

"How was the day?" our mom used to ask us when we would get back from an interview. "Was the interview successful? Did you get the job?"

"No, Mom," we would reply at the same time, disappointed and hurt.

Seeing our disheartened faces, our mother would comfort us. She didn't let us give up. Instead, she would encourage us more and push us to try our best till our last wits, as it was what our father used to believe.

"Do not worry," she would say and stroke our head fondly. "Just keep trying, do not lose hope, and I promise, you will succeed one day!"

And gradually, with the help of some people and our mother's support, my brother and I found a job in a factory. It was a plastic car parts manufacturing company.

The people at the company were really friendly; they not only accepted us but also treated us as if they were their own. I never felt self-conscious or uneasy with them. My manager let me get adjusted to the factory environment and would continuously mentor and train me.

* * *

When I first started working, my English was really bad. I could never give those people enough credit for all the support and help that they gave me. I was a good employee, and my bosses appreciated that. I tried as much as I could to fit in and learn the language as soon as possible.

Some of the coworkers with whom I had become closer helped me learn English. They would teach me the basics of the language, and when I sometimes failed to understand it, they would remain patient and encourage me to try hard.

"I . . . I w-wi-will," I uttered, trying to pronounce a sentence that my senior had written.

"Yes . . . " my senior trailed off supportively.

"Wo . . . rrk ha . . . rd," I said and looked at him, wanting to know if I was right.

He nodded, smiling, and said, "Now, try again and say it in a single sentence."

"I. Will. Work. Hard?" I said, beaming. "Is it right, sir?"

"Yes!" he exclaimed, clapping. "You did it! I knew you could do it!"

And on another occasion, the engineer I worked with would teach me a new word every day. He would let me listen to the radio, and whenever I would hear a word I didn't know, he would explain the meaning to me.

"The new movie released is about a fantasy thriller story about . . ."

"*Fantasy?*" I asked, confused. "What does *fantasy* mean, Mr. Alexander?"

"*Fantasy.*" Alexander paused. "It is something that is not true or exists in reality. It is just something that we have created with our imagination."

In a year, I was able to communicate with them without any problems. My life was a lot better than I had imagined; I found comfort in the new place.

The horrors of my past were still there with me, but I was able to breathe properly this time.

Before coming to America, I initially thought that nobody would accept me, that they would behave just like my neighbors and friends did in Bosnia.

It took some time, but I got accustomed to everything over there. If it weren't for the townspeople, I wouldn't have gotten any courage to get out of my shell.

I made many friends in that town when I first came to Grand Rapids, Michigan, but after some time, I had to move. Even though we are away from each other, I still talk to those people and will never forget them. They are people whom I care deeply about after my family.

To me, Grand Rapids was a small American town that was full of nice and humble people.

Chapter 10

The Second Testimony

I do believe in the old saying, "What does not kill you makes
you stronger." Our experiences, good and bad, make us who
we are. By overcoming difficulties,
we gain strength and maturity.
—Angelina Jolie

The multinational Stabilisation Force (SFOR) arrested Rado on July
9, 2002, and a day later, he was transferred to ICTY. His trial went on for
years until his sentence in 2007.

* * *

By the time Rado was arrested, I was already busy with my life in
America. I didn't know that he was taken into custody until I saw it on
social media. The picture of him being handcuffed and surrounded by the
police was all over the place. Looking at his face again was traumatizing for
me; it made my skin crawl and my body tremble immensely.

A few days later, I learned that witnesses and victims were gathering
around to testify against him. I didn't care much about it and got immersed
in my life. However, one day, while laying my head on my mother's lap,
I questioned myself if I should give my testimony. The thoughts kept
revolving around my mind, frustrating me.

"Child, what are you thinking?" my mother asked, caressing my
head. "Is something troubling you?"

"Mom," I paused, "do you remember Rado? He has surrendered."

"What? When?" she asked, surprised.

"A few days ago," I told her. "I saw a picture of him being escorted by the police."

"What a relief! The person who was leading all this is going to get what he deserves. I hope we all get justice for what those people did to us!"

"Mother, should I go and testify against him?" I inquired, glancing at her.

"It's up to you, child," she said, smiling gently. "If it makes you feel better, then you should. Otherwise, if you don't want to feel insecure, then don't go. But remember, whatever you do . . ." She paused. "Do what you want, not what others want you to do, as it's your life, your battle to fight. No one can understand it better than you."

Talking to my mother was a reality check for me. I realized that I did not want these people to roam the world unharmed. They needed to face the consequences of their horrible deeds. People needed justice. I needed justice. And we wouldn't be getting it until he and all the people involved were behind bars, in pain and suffering.

* * *

It was easier to decide to go to the second trial because I had already been through that experience, and I was older and more mature. The taunting and threats did not upset me anymore; I was brave enough to handle it now.

And also, because I lived in America at that time, I felt much safer, especially since the US Embassy was informed that I was going to Bosnia to testify. I knew and was sure that if something did go wrong in Bosnia, I had people to save me this time.

My cousin that was with me on the first trial was with me on this one as well. She was my supporter and friend; she was why I could go through it without sweating so much. Hearing his name brought a strange feeling, as he was someone close to my family and me. I could not understand how someone could turn out to be like that—and that too, a close friend.

I remember when I was a kid and our family used to have small gatherings. I used to play with him and his siblings. Although he was older than us, we all used to get along well. When I was young and my father was still with us, he and I were friends—at least I thought we were.

Our families had known each other for a long time; my parents trusted them and Rado. They thought of him as an angel who wouldn't get involved in bad things. He was the most respected person in our neighborhood. But alas, it is simply the devil who knows how to camouflage himself from society, hiding his ugly side.

If only my parents and I had known what he would become later on, we wouldn't have stayed far away. My cousin, who was there with me, understood my turmoil and comforted me. She explained that he didn't do it because he had a grudge against me or because it was my fault; it was his decision. It had nothing to do with me.

"Don't ever blame yourself," my cousin commented, eating her porridge while sitting at the breakfast table. "Rado is a traitor for exchanging you with someone else."

"I know." I sighed. "It's just that I feel awful about the whole situation. It is emotional for me. He was like a brother to me. I couldn't understand what had gone wrong for him to behave in that way."

"Sweetheart," my cousin mumbled, taking my hand in hers and squeezing it in assurance, "you don't need to feel sorry. He had chosen that path, he decided to ruin people and himself. It wasn't anyone else's fault."

"Thank you for consoling me," I smiled at her faintly. "Will you accompany me to the testimony?"

"Of course I will! I have promised you that I will always support you, so how can I abandon you now?"

I was pleased that my cousin had been there with me, as testifying against Rado was difficult for me. It was hard for me to understand that somebody I knew and had been friends with could change in a blink of a moment and become a monster.

*　*　*

A day before I had to appear at the court, my cousin decided it would be best for us to clear our minds by stopping at a local market.

We went to a nearby shop that was selling sheets and blankets along with small wooden structures. My mother had always loved handcrafted sheets, and her previous one that my father had given was lost in the war. Knowing that it would cheer her up, I thought of buying two sheets for her.

"What do you think?" my cousin muttered, showing me the blue, circle-patterned blanket in her hand. "The texture is so smooth and soft, don't you think?"

"Yes, I think so," I replied, stroking the blanket's surface. "The color is a vibrant one, I think—"

A hand on my shoulder interrupted me. My eyes widened, and I froze. *Who might that be?* I thought and shakily turned around. A sigh left my mouth, relieved to find a woman standing in front of me.

"Yes, how can I help you?" I questioned, confused. By this time, my cousin came up beside me and stared at the stranger.

"It's me, Petra," she said. "Have you already forgotten your best friend?"

"Oh! Petra?" I exclaimed, shocked to see her there. I squinted my eyes and looked at her closely.

Petra was my high school friend; she used to be very dear to me before the war. We would always share everything with each other. We had a strong bond that couldn't be broken, but things changed after the war started.

A Bosniak accidentally murdered Petra's distant relative. It made her hate every one of us, and she didn't hide it. I was hurt and disappointed to see that she blamed us for everything because of someone's mistake.

When I came back from the detention camp, Petra lied to everyone, calling me names. She would mock and insult me every time.

"What are you doing here?" Petra asked, scowling.

"It's none of your business," my cousin answered. "She can come here whenever she wants to. Who are you to ask her that?"

"I know why you are here," she gritted out. "You are here to testify against Rado, aren't you?" When we didn't say anything, she continued speaking, "Didn't you get satisfied after you testified against Drago? Do you still have more lies to tell? How long will you keep fabricating the truth?"

"Yes, you are right. I am here to testify against Rado," I said calmly, glaring at her. "I don't care what you think of me, you can think whatever you want, but it would not hide the truth!"

"Truth! What is the truth? What are you talking about? You are just lying to degrade us."

"The truth is that I was the victim, along with thousands of girls and women. But it's okay if you don't want to understand." I smiled. "It's all right if you want to live in a false world. I know what they have done and how vile they are. I will fight for justice, and I will only get that after I put them behind bars."

Before she could comment on anything more, my cousin and I moved forward to a different shop to buy sheets. I didn't glance back even after she kept calling my name. I wouldn't let people weaken my resolve and ruin my spirit. I had listened enough to them; their mockery and insults didn't disturb me anymore.

I was not the same naive girl anymore; I had changed. I had my family and friends with me; their love was what made me move on. I knew who I was and what I had gone through, and no one could stop me now from getting them imprisoned!

* * *

The testimony against Rado was more manageable as he was removed from the courtroom because of his bad behavior. He was not able to sit quietly and was commenting on what the witnesses were relating.

"She is lying! She wasn't there! She is just fabricating lies to take revenge on me," I heard him say from the waiting room. His violent screams would terrify the other girls and me.

"You! Who the hell are you? Who do you think you are? If you gave a false statement, I promise I won't leave you alone! I will find you and kill you!"

By the time I was called, he was not there. I was relieved to see this, not knowing what he would've done if he were there.

The testimony was quick because I had met him just a few times and was not in constant contact with him during the war. I explained to the prosecutor how things went on when I was at his mercy.

"When you saw the men at the house at Karman, what were they wearing?" the prosecutor asked me. "Can you please describe to me the color and texture?"

"They were wearing camouflage uniforms," I told her nervously. "I don't remember the specific dress code."

"All right, it's okay," the prosecutor commented. "And what were they doing when you came up to them?"

"T-they were standing there, beside the house. Some of the girls they had dragged with them were coming out of the car and going into the house."

The prosecutor kept asking me question after question. She wanted to know how I figured out that Rado was selling me off to other soldiers.

"You said you saw four girls. What exactly were they doing? When did you see them?"

"I saw them around late in the night, sometime after nine o'clock, I guess."

"Did you see them coming from the car, or did you see them already going into the house? What exactly did you see?"

"I saw them just as they were going into the house. That was the point at which I arrived in front of the house."

"Were you scared at that time?"

"At that time, I didn't know what was going on. So, yes, I was scared."

"What happened next? While the girls entered the house, what did you have to do?"

"Drago and another soldier pushed us toward a black car."

In between the questions, the prosecutor would show me pictures and ask me if I recognized any places. When I had identified all of them, she asked the jury for them to be acknowledged.

At one point, she showed me a picture of Rado and asked me if I could recognize him, and when I did, she asked me how I knew him before the war.

"Rado, did you know him from before the war?"

"Yes, I knew him very well."

"How did you know him?"

"He was my neighbor. We used to live in the same building. He lived on the floor above me."

Answering the questions brought back memories that I had tried so hard to forget. It was the most difficult, to give testimony against him. It was the most emotional testimony because he was my neighbor and I grew up with him.

* * *

Some of the crimes that Rado committed were the following:

Sexual assaults and torture of girls. It was recognized as a crime against humanity and a violation of the laws.

The enslavement of girls in different locations. It was recognized as a crime against humanity.

On September 29, 2005, he was transferred to Bosnia and Herzegovina. And on March 28, 2007, he was sentenced to twenty years of imprisonment.

Chapter 11

The Third Testimony

If you are distressed by anything external, the pain is not due
to the thing itself, but to your estimate of it, and this you have
the power to revoke at any moment.
—Marcus Aurelius

It was in 2005 when Gojo surrendered. He was transferred to ICTY,
where his trials started for the hideous crime he had committed.

* * *

I was in Bosnia giving my testimony for Rado when I was informed
that Gojo had surrendered and was also going through a trial and that
witnesses were also testifying against him. I decided it would be best to
testify against him and go along with my cousin to court.

When I entered the court, I fell; it was as if my legs had no life. But I
got up and decided to go through with it. It took me a while, but I was able
to continue. The first couple of minutes were tormenting, but after that, I
regained my strength and anger.

Why am I feeling embarrassed, and why do I feel like I am not good
enough? I did not do anything, they did. And it is their fault! I thought. I
walked slowly until I reached the witness stand. The prosecutor was already
staring at me, greeting me with a slight nod, ready to ask the dreadful
questions.

It's okay, calm down and relax. I took a deep breath. You can do it, just focus on the prosecutor and the judge, and don't think about anything else!

The prosecutor kept throwing question after question at me. It was making me squirm. I kept pinching my jeans to control myself from shaking.

In the middle of the questioning, Gojo interrupted and asked, "Your Honor, can I ask this girl some questions?"

I was startled by his request. Why would he ask such a thing? And what did he want to ask me? What was he planning? Glancing at the prosecutor and other people, I could see that I wasn't the only one who was surprised.

The judge contemplated his request and, after a second, paused and allowed him to ask me questions.

"You can proceed," she said with a straight face. "But please make sure that you ask questions related to the case. Otherwise, you will face severe consequences."

I was dumbfounded. I was furious at her because she gave him that right. *What is she thinking? Why did she allow him? What is wrong with her?*

"Yes, Your Honor," Gojo said and turned toward me.

Calm down, now is not the time to get furious, I thought. I needed to calm down before he tried to play with my emotions and mind to prove that I was fabricating all this. He wanted to show everyone that I was lying and that I was incompetent.

"How were you there? What did you see over there? What happened? Who made you go through it? Did you see me? Was it me who did all this to you? Where did you see me?" he hollered. "Tell me, who was it? Why are you quiet now?"

I clenched my eyes for a second and exhaled slowly, trying to gain strength. Furiously, I opened my eyes and glared. I felt deep hatred going through my body, and I wanted him to know how much I detested the sight of him. I was going to show him that he and his people could shatter me physically and emotionally, but they could not destroy my willpower. Not now, not ever!

I had had enough of running away from them; now it was my turn to fight back!

"Yes! You were there, and you did all these things!" I screamed, pointing my finger at him. "It was only you. You commanded everything over there."

"I think you saw someone else," he declared, still intent on proving himself innocent. "I don't even know you, so how could you say it was me? I have never seen you before, girl," he stated, feigning. "You have mistaken me for someone else."

"You are wrong, Gojo!" I gritted out. "No, it was not somebody else. IT WAS YOU!"

"Do you know what you are talking about?" he growled slowly, glaring at me. "I don't think so. You are not normal enough to talk right now. You are in delusion!"

I removed every emotion from my face, not letting him see that he could break me again. Taking a long deep breath, I commented, "Yes, you did all this. I am still normal and strong enough to come here, to put you behind bars!" I fisted my hands tightly. "I promise I will make you suffer for what you made small innocent girls go through! For what you made me and my family go through!"

Those guys were counting on us to be scared of them, but they were mistaken. I had nothing to lose, and they could not do anything else to me. I wanted to show him that I was not a kid anymore and that I was still here, stronger than ever, after everything they did to me.

The prosecutor was beside me the moment I stopped talking, consoling me. She was advising me to take a deep breath and calm down.

"It's okay, it's okay," she mumbled. "It's all right, you are doing good. You are one brave woman. Don't get yourself worked up because of someone like him."

"Gojo," the judge commented, "please take your seat."

He nodded and silently went back to his seat. There was a look of satisfaction on his face, knowing that he had shaken me up and shattered my calm exterior. The court session continued, and I answered everything without glancing toward his direction again.

* * *

One of the Serbs from my town tried to threaten me over Facebook. He would harass me continuously, wanting me to back down from giving testimony against Gojo and leave Bosnia before things became unbearable for me.

"I am telling you, leave before you and your family suffer from severe consequences."

"I am not going anywhere. I will give my testimony. He had already damaged many people. He needs to be behind bars before he destroys more life!"

"You are foolish! Gojo is a great man! He is not a monster like you people! He is a hero who is getting punished because of false statements."

"You people are monsters! You made a mistake letting me live," I told him furiously. "You should have killed me before this because now I will not leave you people without getting justice. I will push you people behind bars, I promise."

Before he could say anything, I blocked him. I didn't want to hear from people who wouldn't believe me. They did not care about what we had gone through; they just cared about their people.

I figured that it was useless to fight with them, as explaining to them would not bring back my innocence. It was forever tainted, and the people who were responsible for it needed to get punished.

The tables had been turned.

It was those beasts who were at our mercy now, begging us to help them, that we should think about their family. But did they think about our family? Did they care about what would happen to a family when they were slaughtering the head of the family, the sole breadwinner?

Now I had become stronger than ever and was not afraid of those lowlifes; that was how I saw them. At that time and right now too! I was still alive, and it was not too late for me, but for them, there was nothing left except gloominess and darkness. Their whole life would be spent in a place that would make them regret their life decisions.

I wanted to see them in the same confined place where they had placed me. I had to see them squirm the same way I had when I was imprisoned. I needed to see them broken and abandoned as I had been all those years back. All of them had lost their freedom, their wives and children, and their friends. They did not want to have anything with them; they had lost the respect of many people.

No, they could not rule me anymore. Those people were nothing else but people who were below me. They couldn't destroy my willpower anymore. I would fight with them to get the justice I and many others deserved.

* * *

Some of the crimes that Gojo had committed were the following:

Sexual assaults and torture of girls. It was recognized as a crime against humanity and a violation of the laws.

On December 8, 2005, he was transferred to Bosnia and Herzegovina, and on November 19, 2007, he was sentenced to thirty-four years of imprisonment.

Chapter 12

Nightmares in My Head

If you are lucky enough to find a way of life you love,
you have to find the courage to live it.
—John Irving

Dark, black clouds surrounded me; there wasn't any source of light that could tell me where I was. I peered around and squinted my eyes to see beyond the fog. The chirping of crickets helped me figure out that I was somewhere outside.

But where? And how did I get here?

Slowly, the fog started to disappear, and my vision started to get clearer. Long trees were around me, making me realize that I was in a forest somewhere. There was an eerie silence in the air, except for the occasional chirping of crickets that could be heard.

W-what is going on? I thought, alarmed.

"Hello, i-is someone here?" I shouted, my hoarse voice echoing in the wind.

I sighed in defeat when I didn't receive an answer. I slowly started to wander around, searching for any sign of a human being. The muddy ground was making it hard for me to walk; my feet were getting swallowed.

Halfway through the bushes, I heard a rustle five feet away from my left. I halted in my steps, holding my breath, and waited.

One . . .

Two . . .

Th—

A horrified scream resonated in the air, making goose bumps appear on my body and a shiver go down my spine. It was a girl's voice, and she was screaming somewhere close to me. My instincts told me to run immediately, but I was paralyzed with fear, unable to move.

A few minutes went by in contemplation when suddenly I heard someone running. And the petrifying part was, that person was running in my direction.

Scared that the person might catch me, I started running forward. The person didn't stop; instead, he started chasing me more aggressively. The loud thump of his footsteps made me anxious and nervous, frightened of what would happen if he caught up to me.

"H-help!" I screamed in the air, desperate. "Please, s-someone help me!"

"No one will save you!" the person growled loudly. "I will destroy you!" He laughed.

My legs were getting tired now, and unknowingly, they slowed down. The space between us was decreasing, and he was catching up to me. I could feel his hand was just an inch away from me. Without any warning, a hand caught my shoulder and pulled me back—

Gasp.

I glanced around, frightened. My eyes were wide, and my mouth hung open in shock. I was relieved to find that I was lying on my bed, in my room. I sat up slightly and ran my hands through my hair; sweat was trickling down my forehead.

It was just a dream! No, not a dream but a nightmare!

I sighed, traumatized. It wasn't the first time it happened. I had been having this nightmare for a few months now. The place would be different in every dream, but one thing that remained the same was that someone would be chasing me. But before they could catch me or try to do anything, I would wake up covered in sweat.

It would leave me breathless and worried about the upcoming future. Knowing that I was still terrified of my past, nothing could stop that fear.

I glanced to my left at the side table and groaned when I saw that the water bottle was empty. Swallowing, I made my way downstairs; the lights were off as everyone was sound asleep.

I didn't want to wake up anyone, thinking it would be a burden, so I left the lights off. Patting the walls beside me, I tried to find my way to the kitchen.

As soon as I found it, I rushed toward the cabinet to take out a glass. I opened cabinet after cabinet, rummaging through things, but I could not find any glass.

Where is it? I thought, frustrated. What am I going to do now? What if someone comes? What will they think? I am scared! Please, someone—

"Sister . . . ?" my brother's voice interrupted me, causing me to jump in the air and let out a loud cry. "Sister!" he shouted, panicked, running toward me and embracing me in his arms. He murmured, "It's all right, it's all right. Do not worry, sister. I am here for you. I will fight with anyone for you."

I sobbed immensely, hugging him tightly as if he would disappear in thin air and I would be left alone in the darkness again. My brother continuously caressed my hair and back, giving me comfort. I remained still, crying in my brother's arms for no idea how long.

When I had calmed down, my brother pulled me toward the table and asked me to sit down while he fetched me water. My hands were still trembling, but I hid them under the table as I did not want to show how vulnerable I was.

"Here you go." He pushed the water in my direction. I didn't realize how thirsty I was until I gulped down the whole glass in one go. My brother, seeing that, asked, "More?"

I nodded slightly, and he moved to the counter to grab more. Placing the glass in front of me, he sat down across from me and murmured, "Was it the nightmare again?"

I ceased sipping and stared at him, surprised. How did he know that? I hadn't told anyone that I was having nightmares! So how?

My brother must have understood my expression. He abruptly said, "My room is beside you, sister. I can hear your screams the whole night. I know you were having nightmares, but . . . but I didn't have any courage to ask you about it. And today, when I saw you standing so lost and in despair, I couldn't help myself from asking you."

"Oh!" I uttered and continued to sip the water.

"What was it about? You haven't told us anything you were or are going through," he mumbled, frowning. "If only you could trust us and share your troubles with us. We can help you shoulder it, and you don't have to fight it alone."

I remained quiet, my head lowered and eyes fixated on the wooden table. I couldn't make myself look my brother in the eye; it was too painful for me.

How could a sister tell his brother, a person who was so innocent and kind, about her devastating past? Would he still love me after he learned what I had gone through? I doubt that anyone would love me after knowing my scars.

"It's okay," my brother breathed out. "You don't have to force yourself. You can tell me whenever you think is the right time. I will wait for you." He smiled faintly. "But do know that I will always be there for you when you need a shoulder to cry on. You are not alone anymore, I will be your support from now on."

"Thank you," I whispered, the tears dripping down my eyes one by one.

Only when I could overcome my sufferings would the world become a blissful place for me. But alas, I know it couldn't happen, no matter what I do!

* * *

Once I was walking home from a friend's house late at night when I felt the absence of security in my life. It was around ten o'clock in the night, the streetlights were still on, and the stores were bright with brimming lights.

I loved walking along the streets as I could watch the colors that the world was accustomed to. The fresh air helped me settle down and gave me a sense of power and freedom.

It wasn't until I had crossed the main street and turned toward the alley that I got the uneasy feeling. The alley was dark and daunting, and I realized my mistake. I should have asked my brother to accompany me, or I should have agreed to my friend's father, who had kindly suggested dropping me off.

I was naive. I thought I could cross the path without any hurdles but had forgotten that I had to cross an alley to reach my house!

Moving through the alleys had always been difficult for me; it involuntarily took me to where I was confined years ago. The horror of someone jumping out of a corner haunted me.

Taking a deep breath to calm my nerves, I clenched my hands in a fist and moved forward, taking one step at a time. Constantly, my head moved from right to left, gazing alertly at every corner.

Thud.

I paused and, sucking in a deep breath, slowly turned around. A small, black shadow appeared near the garbage bin. I squinted my eyes to see what it was, but the silhouette moved in a flash.

"Meow."

I screamed and leaped back.

The brown cat moved from behind the bin and stared at me. Dissolving in tears, I slid down to the floor and sobbed.

Why did it happen to me? When will I be brave enough not to get frightened of small things? When will the fear stop?

My phone rang, and I hurriedly lifted it to see who was calling. I smiled when I saw that my friend was calling me to know if I had reached home safely. I pondered for a few seconds if I should tell her that I was lost. Irritated and worn out, I gave up and picked up the call, relating the incident to her.

* * *

On one occasion, my mother told me how differently I was behaving. It distressed them to see me this disturbed and terrified. It happened on a Friday morning when my family and I were peacefully listening to the radio.

We were listening to a song, enjoying the lyrics and humming along with it.

"Isn't that your favorite song, sister?" my youngest brother asked me.

"Yes, it is," I told him, pinching his cheeks.

"Why do you like it so much?" he sulked. "It isn't really that good."

We all laughed, finding his sulking adorable.

"Two days ago, at a house near the national park, a woman was abused and beaten by her husband . . ." The radio continued, but my mind was fixated on the sentence.

"I couldn't believe it! How can someone do this to anyone?" my brother grumbled. "I wonder how people can do that to women, I can never raise a hand on a woman."

"There are many people like that, brother!" my youngest brother said. "I always hear these things from my friends."

"How disturbing was the incident, isn't it, sister?" my brother turned toward me and stilled. "Sister?" He moved toward me and said, "Sister, are you all right?"

This turned everyone's attention toward me, and my brother lightly placed his hand on my shoulder and said, "Sister, what is the problem? Are you—"

"Don't come near me!" I shrieked and backed away from his hand.

My mother and brothers were startled; they stared at me wide-eyed.

"Child?" my mother called out, moving slowly toward me.

"Please, please!" I wailed, falling to the floor on my knees. "Please leave me alone! I won't say anything to anyone, just please let me go! I beg you, please, let me live and go back to my family!"

My loved ones were there beside me, crying for me, but I was so deep in that space that I could not respond to them.

* * *

My family and friends were worried when they heard about the nightmares and the incidents. They didn't know what the cause behind it was, but they could understand that it was something severe and unbearable.

My friend insisted that I go for a therapy session as she believed it would help me overcome my fears. I refused it, afraid of people judging me and calling me names.

"But why?" she asked, scowling. "It will be beneficial for you, dear."

"I don't want anyone to know," I mumbled. "It makes me remember the horrible incidents."

"But then, how will you move in your life? Don't you want to live your life without worrying that someone would destroy it?" She sighed heavily. "Psychologists help people recover from their traumas, they do not judge people for who or what they are. You need to face your fears head-on."

Years passed, but I didn't meet a psychologist. In fact, whenever I heard people talking about therapies, I would flee from that place.

Why was it hard for people to understand that my life wasn't simple? It had been shattered already; nothing or no one could help me collect the pieces. I wasn't brave enough to share my burdens with other people.

It was not until 2018 that I gathered myself and decided to go for a therapy session. I am still going through it, and I know that I will probably stay in therapy for a long time.

My therapist became my best friend; I was comfortable sharing my sorrows with her. I was lucky to find a nice therapist, and I made a connection with her instantly. She had been the only person that I could talk to about anything and not get judged for it.

The day I met her had been etched on my mind and heart. And right away, we clicked with each other as if we had known each other for ages.

She didn't make me uncomfortable, and I was able to tell her about my traumas without worrying that she would criticize me.

"Hello," the psychologist said, smiling warmly at me. "Please make yourself comfortable, and then we can start the session."

I was nervous at that time; sweat beads were forming on my forehead. My eyes would move around the room in anxiousness, dreading my decision.

"Yes, dear," she said. "Now, please slowly tell me about yourself and what is troubling you."

"I lived with my family in Bosnia . . ."

Steadily, I began to tell her about myself and what happened during the war. Whenever I would hesitate, she would nod in encouragement, and I would continue.

I started to get relaxed and less anxious. I was alleviated to know there was no expression of disgust or remorse on her face. Instead, her expressions remained neutral throughout the session.

I was supposed to start therapy a long time ago, but I was afraid and ashamed to admit that I had problems in my life. It took me a while to open up as sharing those life experiences drained me and weakened my will.

Once a week, I would take individual therapy with my psychologist to address my mental health.

My current clinical diagnoses are high anxiety, chronic post-traumatic stress disorder (PSTD), and mild but recurrent major depressive disorder (MDD).

My therapist and I would perform EMDR therapy to overcome my PTSD. EMDR treatment is a therapy that works in a cycle; it is a way to deal with the traumas and different indicators by reconnecting to the damaged person in a secure and calculated manner.

It helped me connect the depictions, reflections, and distressing feelings that were related to the incident and helped my brain to heal normally.

Although it was hard to adapt to in the beginning, I slowly became comfortable with the therapy sessions. It became a part of my life, and I started becoming less ashamed of myself.

With therapy, I learned that my mental health was as necessary as my physical health. I would not be able to get back to my life until I tackled the issues I had trapped in my mind.

I was not a person who was ill or needed attention. I was someone who needed to heal from her traumas. And with time, I would accomplish it!

* * *

The trials and tortures had ended, but the agony still remained. They didn't leave me; they followed me until I had fully succumbed to darkness, which swallowed me.

The voice of my tormentors, their laughing faces, would haunt me again and again. They were stuck in my head as how a centipede attaches itself to a human being, not leaving them until they leave behind a poisonous bite.

I was getting better, but I still had a lot of issues. I used to have nightmares, and they were always the same, but after the therapy sessions, they did not appear as often as had before because I had been taking medication for anxiety and nightmares.

I was still afraid of dark and small spaces, especially when I was confined in a room and there was no light. It became so distressing to me that at some point, I would collapse and weep until there were no tears left.

I did not like to be alone as it took me back to the days when the monsters used to torture me and I did not have the chance of being with somebody I could trust. I had been abused and misused so many times before that trusting people became hard for me.

People kept abusing me and saying horrible things about me. Yet I was unable to stop them. How could somebody have the ability to break someone's will into tiny pieces? What gave them the power to make other people's life hell?

I was in constant fear that I would somehow lose people that were dear to my heart. My family did not know as much because I tried to keep all the problems to myself as much as I could. I never wanted to trouble them, especially when they had already suffered a lot.

My mother was at the age where knowing about these things would tear her apart. She was still mourning for my father; I didn't want her to also grieve for her daughter, who was a shell without life.

The wounds were still fresh when I started getting back to my life. Even after so many years had passed, there was still an unnerving feeling at the back of my head that stopped me from moving forward in life.

Over the years, I wondered when the dark, gloomy clouds would fade away from my life and when the bright sun would appear again. It was an impossible hope, but somewhere in my mind, I believed that the day would come.

It just needed some time.

At a certain point in my life, I would heal, not completely but enough that it won't bother me anymore.

Chapter 13

New Beginnings

That's what people who love you do. They put their arms
around you and love you when you're not so lovable.
—Deb Caletti

In those most challenging times of my life, my family was always there beside me, to support me and cheer for me. They would do their best to make things bearable and sufficient for me.

I had experienced and acknowledged that people would change according to the situation. They would leave you as soon as they found something they didn't like.

Everyone except our family.

They would stick with us, go through what we've gone through, and fight with us in the long run. They won't abandon us or make us feel ashamed. Instead, they would never let go of our hand but rather hold it tightly.

It was painful for me to see my family walking on glass shells around me for years. They were trying to dodge things and people who might hurt me or cause me trouble.

It was a difficult phase of my life. I had to learn things about my family again, which I missed in the years I was away from them.

Over the years, things started to look clearer and more pleasant. I began to enjoy my life and was thankful that I was alive despite the disturbing events I had gone through.

Relationships were not a part of my life. I had long given up on dating and loving someone. After my last awful relationship, I found it difficult to open up with people. There was a constant reminder at the back of my mind that not many people would accept me; they would find ways to reject or degrade me.

And I was okay with that.

I didn't need a lot of people in my life; my family and close-knit friends were all I needed.

With that thought, I moved on in my life without having a clue that someone would come into my life and make it more beautiful. A person who would stay beside me firmly and would not care about the consequences. The one who would become my biggest supporter, my husband.

Initially, I rejected his proposal, but my husband was persistent in being with me. He would try to make things comfortable for me and resort to doing things I felt happier about.

I would overhear people questioning him on what attracted him to me and what was appealing about me that he was willing to wait.

I thought about that too. I was just a plain Jane; why would he even like an ordinary girl?

I had difficulty getting comfortable with him. I would get flashbacks of the past years whenever he would try to know more about me. My experience left me so repulsed by men that even if they meant no harm, I would jump away from them.

But my husband was patient throughout everything, letting me know that he was always there for me.

"It's okay, love," he would say every time, with a gentle smile. "I will wait for you, even if it takes forever. You don't need to force yourself for anything."

And little by little, I didn't realize when, but he started to take place in my heart. I was thankful for his caring and loving nature, which had been consistent until now. But there was a disturbing thought in my mind: What if he left me after learning about everything? Would he still love me the same way he did? Or would he be repulsed by the unpleasant scars I have on me?

As the fears increased, I became more anxious. My husband, who had always been mindful of his surroundings, would know when something was troubling me. But the best thing about him was that he would never force me to tell him anything. Instead, he would be considerate and wait patiently.

And eventually, after much contemplation and apprehension about losing him, I told him about my life. I didn't leave anything out. I relayed my story to him in detail, going through the three agonizing scars of my life.

"I . . . I . . ." I sobbed loudly, lowering my head in my hand, hiding my face from him. "I am covered with dirt, those obnoxious scars would never leave me. It will get deeper the more I try to clean it."

He remained quiet; I couldn't understand what was going on in his mind at that time. I became apprehensive when he just stood there; I wanted to know what he was thinking, what he felt, and if he still loved me wholeheartedly.

Yet I didn't look up in his direction as I did not dare to look into his eyes. Devastated that he would back down, I bit my lips to suppress the scream that wanted to come out and swallowed hard.

I told you not to get attached to any guy, you silly girl! Look where it got you! Isolated and unhappy! You are not worth the love! People were right, you don't deserve to be loved!

The thoughts kept resonating around me, shattering my will and soul completely, proving to me that I was wrong to assume that he would love me. I was so lost in thoughts that I did not realize when two rough hands on my shoulder pulled me out of my despair.

"Hey!" he called. "What is going on? Why are you trembling so hard?"

"Huh!" I murmured, glancing at him, surprised.

"What is troubling you?" he asked, worried. "Did I do something wrong? Did I hurt you? Tell me, please, I want to know what is making you upset."

"I . . . I . . . ," I stammered, confused. "D-don't you feel r-repulsed by me? I know that I am not worthy enough to get your love." I paused, exhaling slowly, and gazed at him. "Don't worry, I won't hold you off. You are free to go and move on with your life. I won't blame you."

"Are you done, or do you want to say something more?" he asked firmly.

Startled, I glanced at his eyes and was shocked to see that he had a determined expression on his face. His face was stern, letting me know that he was firm on whatever decision he had made.

I nodded shakily.

"Good," he said and placed his hand on my face. Smiling softly, he murmured, "I don't know from where you got this absurd idea in your mind, but let me tell you one thing, I am not going anywhere and will love you till the end." He spelled out each word, once again reassuring me, "I. Am. Not. Leaving. You."

"W-wait, what?"

"It was not your fault. The horrendous things you had to go through were not your fault but theirs," he said, tearing up. "And please, you are not covered in dirt. You are a virtuous woman, and you will always be perfect for me."

The tears that were brimming in my eyes began to flow excessively. I was delighted to hear him. I couldn't believe that someone was persistent in being with me after knowing everything.

I remember the first time I let my family meet my husband. It was a tense situation as, after the incident, my family had become protective of me, especially my brothers.

It took them more than ten visits to get comfortable around each other. They began to consider my husband as family and were happy that I had found a loving person.

The other day, when I was on the patio, my brother came and sat beside me on the wooden bench. He had a vibrant smile on his face and was gazing up at the sky. I could understand that he wanted to have a conversation with me.

"What is it?" I inquired, glancing at him.

"Nothing, just . . . ," he said, smiling and glancing at me from the corner of his eyes.

I raised an eyebrow in question and said, "I am your big sister. I know what is going on in your mind. You can never hide it, nor can you fool me."

"Oh really?" he chuckled.

"Yes, now tell me." I paused, gazing at him. "Is it about him?"

"Oh gosh!" he exclaimed. "Yes, it is." He grinned and turned toward me. "I . . . I am just glad you are finally with a person who is worthy of your love. That guy is a nice person. I could see that he loves you completely."

"Thank you. I am happy that you people like him."

"Why wouldn't we? We want to see you happy and relaxed in your life, and if that person makes you happy, then we are also happy."

We both smiled.

"Remember, I told you that one day you will find the person who will love you for who you are. And see you finally did. I am happy for you, sister." My brother beamed.

Little by little, things began to go back to normal. My husband and I became closer, and our relationship got stronger. I would tell him everything without any hesitation, aware that he would not judge me in any way.

My brother was right. My husband accepted me the way I was, and he didn't complain about anything. He loved me while I was covered with those hideous scars.

I used to hear from some of my colleagues and friends how their partners would mock or insult their past when involved in arguments. They would tell me how their partners would belittle them in everything and make fun of their hardship, calling them names and accusing them of lying.

At that moment, I would feel blessed that I was in the company of a man who never judged me. In fact, whenever I would feel ashamed and call myself awful, he would tell me, "You are beautiful, love. And not only that but your soul and heart too. Your soul was what made me fall for you in the first place, dear."

I learned with the help of my family and friends that I was not worthless. My husband would often tell me that he was blessed to have me as his wife and was proud of me.

Somewhere deep down, I had self-loathing. I was disgusted by my existence. I would have kept on hating myself if my husband had not shown me what self-love was. He helped me understand that I should not be hard on myself as whatever had happened was beyond my control.

The scars that had all the time reminded me of dreadful episodes do not affect me anymore. I have learned to own it; they are what define me, a part of me.

I had been spending my life in fear, worrying about whether someone recognized me and went after me. The worst would be if those people harm my family and friends in any way.

I used to glance back over my shoulder every time I crossed the streets. I was wary of people; their kindness seemed to me as if they were pretending to be good.

I realized I was terrified whenever those old apprehensions went through my mind and I would remember my old friends' insulting taunts. I was lost and terrified for many years, trapped in the same place.

I realized I was frightened when these terrible memories would set themselves free from their chains and attack my certainty, disintegrating what I had worked on for these past years.

The fear would come mostly in the shape of nightmares when I would be worn out and tired. But by the time I woke up, they would escape, confusing me if I had just imagined them or if they really happened.

There have been lots of incidents where I would start crying and run away from the place. People would try to confront me, trying to know what was wrong. But I would keep a distance from them.

I used to have low self-esteem, and I would blame myself for everything for a long time. But not now. I am getting better because of my therapist, family, and most importantly, my loving husband.

I understand that I was the victim, not the other way around. I should not be ashamed or guilty of what happened in my life. It wasn't in my hand, nor was it my will that those incidents occurred in my life.

> You must make a decision that you are going to move on.
> It won't happen automatically. You will have to rise and say,
> I don't care how hard this is, I don't care how disappointed
> I am, I'm not going to let this get the best of me.
> I'm moving on with my life.
> —Joel Osteen

Imagine hiking on a dangerous rocky mountain on a cold winter night. Alone and far away from society. We would come across different hurdles while trying to reach the top of the hill.

Sometimes we would fall and hurt our legs. At times, we would find it tiring and exhausting, which would push us to give up. And at times, we would be forced to starve in the cold and windy environment.

The barriers would stop us from moving on to our goal. They would make things painful and also hard to breathe. But no matter what, to reach our distinguished goal, we must keep going until we reach the goal.

Our life struggle is similar to hiking; things or people would become obstacles and prevent us from living a good life. They would make things harder for us that would sometimes destroy our souls.

We should never forget that we must not submit to them and move forward without caring about what they think.

Yes, we all go through tough times, and sometimes we feel like there is no hope, but nothing can last forever. There will always be hope somewhere. It might not come to us immediately, but it will be there for us one day. We need to be patient and believe in it.

Throughout those struggles, it's really important to remember to stay sane as only that would help us get through those trying times. We should not succumb to the darkness but fight it immensely.

There may be specific times in our life when we feel disappointed and upset. In those moments, we think about leaving everything we have worked hard for.

The question is, why? Why do we do that? Is our effort worth nothing that we decide to abandon it because of some obstacle?

I have learned from my experiences that we people go through difficulties to become who we are. It is what makes us stronger and more courageous.

Life will throw hurdles in our way, but we must not back away, nor shall we lose hope. We must fight back to reach our goals and dreams.

The hurdles do not only mean things; they could be people as well. The world consists of both the best and worst human beings. We encounter both of them.

The good ones are the ones who will always stay with us, no matter the result. They would find solutions to be there for us. They are the ones who would support us throughout our tough times.

The worst ones are the ones who would leave us in a vulnerable moment. They will shatter and destroy our goodwill and will also make us feel worthless.

The most important thing to remember is that there will always be good people everywhere. Even if things go astray, we should remember that there will always be someone out there who will love us for who we are, not for what people define us. Such a person will be with us through thick and thin.

Fear is a part of our life; there will be some times when we have to go through things that make us scared. Everyone behaves differently at that time; some run away to save themselves while others freeze up.

The crucial thing is to know how to overcome these fears and challenges and face them confidently. And for that, we need to figure out what made us fearful in the first place and how it started.

Our path is to move forward through those difficulties. I know it isn't simple, but it is worth it.

We should love ourselves and not let people have the power to break our spirit. Also, recollect that we are loved. From that point will come our solidarity and the light of triumph ahead.

With the help of this book, I wanted to share my experience with people who are suffering from uncalled-for things. I wanted to convey that we are all together in this, and you are not alone.

As healing is essential in our lives, we need to let go of things to help us move on and enjoy our lives with our loved ones. Keeping grudges and taking revenge will not bring back our lost time; rather, it will always keep us in a bitter place.

Know that the people who have wronged us will get their karma one day. We will receive justice one day.

Epilogue

The warm wind was blowing toward the balcony, ruffling my hair in the air. It sent a shiver down my spine, leaving behind a sweet sensation. My hands tightened on the railing in agitation.

The illuminating moon was making the dark sky gleam in the night. The stars that were playing hide-and-seek with the big, gray clouds teasingly came out and winked at the busy street.

I gazed down at the lively streetside, where vehicles were zooming past in a blink. The tiny yellow, white, and red lights shining on the road had always fascinated me. I enjoyed gazing at them as the colors allowed me to have a soothing and peaceful atmosphere.

"Dear . . . ?" I heard a voice behind me. Involuntary, a smile appeared on my lips, and I looked over my shoulder to my husband, leaning on the sliding door. "Why are you out here, alone? The birthday party is about to start."

"I wanted some fresh air," I told him and looked back toward the street.

He came forward and stood beside me, gazing out front. We stood there for a while, lost in our thoughts. My husband turned toward me and murmured, "Is something troubling you?"

"No, nothing is . . ." I took a pause, contemplating. "Actually, there is, but I don't know how to explain it to you."

"Take your time." He looked at me and smiled gently.

"I don't know what to do. I am going to visit Dad's grave in two days. I-it's been so long since he had left our side, but it always feels like he is there with us at one moment and the next he isn't. I just . . . I just miss Dad a lot."

Heavy silence fell between us.

My husband had never pressured me to tell him anything; he just waited patiently until I told him what was troubling me. He would sometimes also leave me alone so that I could recollect my unsettling thoughts.

"I . . . I . . ." I swallowed hard. "I am just nervous that it is the first time in twenty-nine years that I am going to the city where I was imprisoned."

"Hmm . . . I can understand what you are distressed about." He sighed. "You are worried that you may remember things that you have tried to forget."

"Yeah," I muttered. "It was too traumatizing."

Placing his right hand on my left one, he squeezed it and whispered, "Everything will be all right, you are the bravest girl I know, and I know you are strong enough to fight anything. So just relax, take a deep breath, and let fate help you flow in the right direction."

"All right," I said. "And—"

"Sister!" my younger brother's loud voice can be heard from downstairs. "Brother-in-law! Where are you both? We are going to cut the cake!"

My husband chuckled beside me, and extending his right hand toward me, he blurted out, "Let's go before he wakes up the neighbors."

I laughed, clasping his hand, and nodded.

* * *

People were moving in different directions, running toward their destinations. Booming laughter and the sound of chatter were enveloping me. Everyone in that place was in high spirits, ready to start a journey they had long been waiting for.

I smiled and waved at the infant boy, who was making hand gestures and giggling in my direction. Seeing the little interaction, his mother smiled warmly at me.

"Here is your cappuccino." A large cup of coffee suddenly appeared in my vision. I looked from the hand holding the cup, to the arm, and finally, to my cousin's vibrant smile. My brothers were standing behind her.

"Thank you," I muttered, smiling and taking the hot, steaming cup from her.

Taking a sip, the bittersweet and creamy texture of the coffee helped calm me down. My cousin sat beside me, a bagel and a mocha in her hands. My youngest brother was on a call with our mother while my younger brother sat on my right side.

He looked at me and smiled faintly. He murmured, "Are you nervous?"

"Yes, I am," I muttered softly. "I don't know how I will face people. What if . . . what if I encounter old neighbors and friends over there, brother?"

"Don't fret about it any longer. I promise nothing will go wrong, sister." He grabbed my hand and squeezed it. "You can do it! We all are here for you."

I nodded and squeezed back.

"We can do it," my youngest brother mumbled, placing his hand on top of ours. "Father is waiting for us."

"Me too," my cousin commented, also placing her hand on ours, comforting us.

I glanced at each of their faces, smiling at them through my teary eyes, and they beamed back widely at me. In that instant, I remembered my husband's words of reassurance and gained strength from them.

"Good afternoon, passengers. This is the boarding announcement for flight A5 to Bosnia . . ."

The announcer's voice interrupted us, snapping us out of the moment and prompting us to board the flight. We started to make our way to the terminal, my brothers in front pushing our luggage carts, with my cousin walking behind them.

My steps faltered, and I glanced back at the clear sky from the lounge window.

Here we go! I smiled and followed them.

Acknowledgements

Special thanks to my friend Alyese Faibisoff who helped me with this book and encouraged me to tell my story.

I thank my mother who endured everything alone. She was left alone with three small children and managed to guide all three of us on the right path. Mom, I love you so much, and I'm here for you always.

Of course, I give great gratitude to my greatest support, my husband Mirza.

A big thank you to my brothers Samir and Damir, my sister-in-law Jasmina, sister-in-law Naza, my sister-in-law Belma, and my brother-in-law Denijal who were with me and went with me through my mood swings and all my fears.

Special thanks to my nieces Medina and Ena and nephews Medin, Mirnes, Amar, and Elmin.

I owe special thanks to my cousin Dr. Sabina Galijatovic who was with me at all the trials and who was my biggest support in the most difficult moments and who has remained my support to this day. I also owe a great deal of gratitude to her husband Mustafa Galijatovic. I love you both and thank you for everything.

And of course, I thank my therapist Mada Leanga who is a great help and support to me. Thank you for your understanding and help. Thank you for being always on my side and for helping me to respect and love myself once again

I would like to thank all the people from The Hague Tribunal who were there to facilitate the witnesses.

I would like to thank my friends Lindim, Albiana, Mirsad, Mina, and Dina who have been with me all this time and have accepted me with all my flaws and virtues.

I owe my gratitude to the wonderful people from Michigan, who accepted me and helped me learn English and helped me integrate into American society.

About the Author

Amra Podrug Kratina was born in Foca, Bosnia and Herzegovina, on October 28, 1975.

www.ingramcontent.com/pod-product-compliance
Lightning Source LLC
Chambersburg PA
CBHW030915140626
46545CB00017B/2370